Seek Ye First

Seek Ye First

Joel S. Goldsmith

Edited by
Lorraine Sinkler

Acropolis Books, Publisher
Atlanta, Georgia

For information contact:
ACROPOLIS BOOKS, INC.
Atlanta, Georgia

www.acropolisbooks.com

Library of Congress Cataloging-in-Publication Data

Goldsmith, Joel S., 1892-1964.
  Seek ye first / Joel S. Goldsmith ; edited by Lorraine Sinkler.
    p. cm.
Includes bibliographical references.
  1. New Thought. 2. Spiritual life. I. Sinkler, Lorraine. II. Title.

BF639 .G56885 2002
299'.93--dc21

                            2002014966

Except the Lord build the house,
they labour in vain that build it. . .

– Psalm 127

⌐

"Illumination dissolves all material ties and binds men together with the golden chains of spiritual understanding; it acknowledges only the leadership of the Christ; it has no ritual or rule but the divine, impersonal universal Love; no other worship than the inner Flame that is ever lit at the shrine of Spirit. This union is the free state of spiritual brotherhood. The only restraint is the discipline of Soul; therefore, we know liberty without license; we are a united universe without physical limits, a divine service to God without ceremony or creed. The illumined walk without fear – by Grace."

–*The Infinite Way* by Joel S. Goldsmith

Dedication

Twentieth century mystic Joel S. Goldsmith revealed to the Western world the nature and substance of mystical living that demonstrated how mankind can live in the consciousness of God. The clarity and insight of his teachings, called the Infinite Way, were captured in more than thirty-five books and in over twelve hundred hours of tape recordings that, today, perpetuate his message.

Joel faithfully arranged to have prepared from his class tapes, monthly letters which were made available as one of the most important tools to assist students in their study and application of the Infinite Way teachings. He felt each of these letters came from an ever-new insight that would produce a deeper level of understanding and awareness of truth as students worked diligently with this fresh and timely material.

Each yearly compilation of the *Letters* focused on a central theme, and it became apparent that working with an entire year's material built an ascending level of consciousness. The *Letters* were subsequently published as books, each containing all the year's letters. The publications became immensely popular as they proved to be of great assistance in the individual student's development of spiritual awareness.

Starting in 1954, the monthly letters were made availiable to students wishing to subscribe to them. Each year of the *Letters* was published individually during 1954 through 1959 and made available in book form. From 1960 through 1970 the *Letters* were published and renamed as books with the titles:

1960 Letters	*Our Spiritual Resources*
1961 Letters	*The Contemplative Life*
1962 Letters	*Man Was Not Born to Cry*
1963 Letters	*Living Now*
1964 Letters	*Realization of Oneness*
1965 Letters	*Beyond Words and Thoughts*
1966 Letters	*The Mystical I*
1967 Letters	*Living Between Two Worlds*
1968 Letters	*The Altitude of Prayer*
1969 Letters	*Consciousness Is What I Am*
1970 Letters	*Awakening Mystical Consciousness*

Joel worked closely with his editor, Lorraine Sinkler, to ensure each letter carried the continuity, integrity, and pure consciousness of the message. After Joel's transition in 1964, Emma A. Goldsmith (Joel's wife) requested that Lorraine continue working with the monthly letters, drawing as in the past from the inexhaustible tape recordings of his class work with students. The invaluable work by Lorraine and Emma has ensured that this message will be preserved and available in written form for future generations. Acropolis Books is honored and privileged to offer in book form the next eleven years of Joel's teaching.

The 1971 through 1981 *Letters* also carry a central theme for each year, and have been renamed with the following titles:

1971 Letters	*Living by the Word*
1972 Letters	*Living the Illumined Life*
1973 Letters	*Seek Ye First*
1974 Letters	*Spiritual Discernment: the Healing Consciousness*
1975 Letters	*A Message for the Ages*
1976 Letters	*I Stand on Holy Ground*
1977 Letters	*The Art of Spiritual Living*
1978 Letters	*God Formed Us for His Glory*
1979 Letters	*The Journey Back to the Father's House*
1980 Letters	*Showing Forth the Presence of God*
1981 Letters	*The Only Freedom*

Acropolis Books dedicates this series of eleven books to Lorraine Sinkler and Emma A. Goldsmith for their ongoing commitment to ensure that these teachings will never be lost to the world.

Table of Contents

Seek Ye First

Chapter One

The Inner Kingdom

I turned to speak to God
About the world's despair;
But to make bad matters worse
I found God wasn't there.

God turned to speak to me
(Don't anybody laugh)
God found I wasn't there —
At least not over half.

Robert Frost

It is folly to go to God to ask God to stop war, to feed the starving peoples of the world, to do something about the horrible conditions on earth. Through thousands of years of that kind of praying, it has been discovered that God is not listening to our appeals to do something on earth. God is not listening to us. No, instead we should be listening to God. God is eternally speaking. All around the clock God is speaking to man. There is never a moment in which the still small voice is not being uttered, but as Robert Frost observes, we are not there, at least not half of the time and probably not half of us.

Listening, a State of Receptivity

The essence of the spiritual life lies in the hearing of the still small voice: the ability to receive impartations from God, to be taught of God, to receive God's grace. Most of us have done the reverse of that by speaking to God, telling God, trying to influence God, whereas there is no God listening. In the degree that we have the hearing ear, however, and can feel within ourselves a receptivity to the Spirit, are we God-governed. When Paul refers to "the natural man who receiveth not the things of the Spirit of God,"[1] he certainly must be referring to the man who is talking to God, telling or asking God, and when he speaks of the children of God "who are heirs of God,"[2] he must be speaking of those who have learned to be still:

Be still, and know that *I*, the Spirit
at the center of your being, is God. Be still,
and let It impart Itself to you. Be still!
In quietness and confidence, receive God's grace.*

Since we have had all these centuries of reversed living, we naturally find that it is difficult to begin the spiritual way of life and become immersed in it. For this reason the first few months or the first year of living this life are difficult. In fact, it must be expected that it be difficult because we are embarking on an almost impossible task, that is, unless our determination is such that we are willing to put up with the difficulties inevitably to be encountered in the beginning.

---

* Spontaneous meditations came to Joel during periods of uplifted consciousness and are not in any sense intended to be used as affirmations, denials, or formulas. They have been inserted from time to time to serve as examples of the free flowing of the Spirit. As the reader practices the Presence, he, too, in exalted moments, will receive ever new and fresh inspiration as the outpouring of the Spirit. —Ed.

Forgiveness and Salvation Now

In the years devoted to this work, I have noted some things that are helpful to students and that make these first months easier. One is the practice or technique having to do with the word *now*. To understand this, let us begin with the assumption that there is nothing we can do about our past. Regardless of how scarlet our past may have been or may be right up to this moment, regardless of how lacking in an interest in God, regardless of the sins of omission or commission, if we had to do it over again it would not be that way, or that whatever it is we have done or not done has been through ignorance.

If we must find a scapegoat, let us not blame it on a person, not even on ourselves; let us blame it on our ignorance of the spiritual way and have done with it. Let us end it, because at this moment nothing more can be done about it than truly to feel regret, repentance over our past, and then say, "What now?"

The woman taken in adultery and forgiven by the Master had to accept her forgiveness *now* and stop living in the past. The thief on the cross had to accept his salvation *now* and forget those things that were behind. So must we, regardless of the nature or the degree of our materialistic living, sickly, sinful, or poverty-stricken living. There comes a time when we bid it goodbye and start over with the word *now,* and let *now* mark the beginning of our new birth.

Dropping the Burdens of the Past

Now, here where I am, God is.
Now God is; now God is closer than breathing;
now the Father is saying, "Son, thou art ever
with me, and all that I have is thine."[3]

In this moment of silent receptivity, the Father says,
"Drop your burdens, let Me carry the load. Let Me

give you forgiveness, let Me be the bread,
the meat, the wine, and the water of life.
Drop your burdens at My feet now."

Let us not go back into the past: let us drop these burdens now, and let us acknowledge that *I* in the midst of us is the Christ, *I* in the midst of us is the bread, meat, wine, and water.

I am to be fed now by the spirit of God within me.
I am to be clothed and housed now by the
spirit of God within me. My business is to
be prospered, not by might or by power,
but by the spirit of God that is within me.

Now, in this moment, we must drop our burdens. That means to realize that there is an inner Presence, an inner Power that is manifesting Itself in our daily affairs.

Inner Awareness of the One Father Brings an Outer Unitedness

In many ways the world is getting closer to the one world envisioned by Wendell Wilkie, that day in which nations will unite their business interests instead of making them so completely competitive. They will so arrange their currencies that the currencies of all the world will have equal value. The great airlines are uniting to give greater efficiency in management and economize on expense. Some of the Protestant churches are coming together in a growing ecumenical movement. The era of one world is coming closer and closer.

As students on the spiritual path, however, we have to go a step further and realize that even though the outer world may be united into one world, at this particular stage of unfoldment there are two worlds. There is this outer world of men, women, places, and things, gradually coming together through an evolution of human consciousness, but there is also an inner world in which we are already united and are already one. There is neither Jew nor Greek in the inner world; there is neither white nor black; there is neither foreign nor domestic; there is neither Occidental nor Oriental in that kingdom of God within us because there is but one Father. "Call no man your father upon the earth: for one is your Father, which is in heaven,"[4] one creative Principle. He has made us in His image and likeness, and that means all of us.

In this inner kingdom we are already united, and it is the worldwide recognition of this today that is making possible a measure of unitedness in the outer world. If it had not been for this past century in which men and women have been awakening more and more to the reality of this inner world and their oneness in it, the world would not be ready for this outer uniting.

What takes place within us in our inner world governs our outer world. In other words, our outer conduct is governed by what takes place in our inner world. Let us experiment with that idea for a moment by turning within:

"I and my Father are one."[5] I call no man my father upon
the earth for there is but One: the Father within.

My Father is your Father; your Father is my Father;
there is only one spiritual creative Principle,
and It has created us as members of one household.
We are one in spiritual sonship.

The sense of separateness is discarded, and we are united in the realization that we have but one spiritual Father and that therefore all of our acquaintances are of that same household, brothers and sisters in spiritual sonship. We can extend that awareness to the whole world in this moment of awareness. How can bias, bigotry, or hate remain in such a consciousness? No one can say, "Oh, I am tolerant," because no one is tolerant and, what is more important, no one is understanding until he has come to an actual realization of the fatherhood of God and the brotherhood of man. He might be tolerant in the sense of tolerating somebody, but that is not the understanding needed on earth for unitedness. Oneness requires the understanding of the one Father, the one household, the brotherhood of man.

A Higher Form of Prayer and Spiritual Living

We are fulfilling the greatest law of the Bible when we are loving our neighbor as ourselves. There is no other way to love our neighbor as ourselves except to accept him into our family, into our heart, and into our prayers. How different is the relationship that exists on earth the moment we have united with our fellow men under the fatherhood of God. This is love, not spoken love, but love in action. This is what I mean when I speak of prayer without words and without thoughts.

We are praying without words and without thoughts the moment we close our eyes and accept God as the universal creative Principle and all men as offspring of that one Source. We can do this without thinking it; we can do this without saying it: we can feel it. We can feel love by acknowledging the fatherhood of God and the brotherhood of man, feel the love that goes out to all mankind once we have realized the spiritual nature of man's being and our common Source. This is a higher form of prayer than words or thoughts. This is loving our neighbor as ourselves, and it is the highest form of spiritual living that we can experience until we come into the actual union with God.

Living in the Nowness of Our New Birth

It is important to drop our past, let go of it, and to accept God as the universal Father and mankind as the universal brotherhood. And this must be done in the now. Our entire past of unlovingness is wiped out; all the karma we may have stored up by our hates, envyings, jealousies, bigotries, and biases is wiped out in this moment of now. There is no longer a past: there is only now, " now are we the sons of God"[6]; now are we united in the bonds of brotherhood. In this recognition of now, we have begun the new birth. The old man "dies"; the new man of love is born.

Our function from now on is to live in a continuing sense of nowness so that whether we are walking out on the street or attending to our business or home duties, regardless of what we may be doing with the mind and the body, we must reserve an area of consciousness in which we recognize the fatherhood of God and the brotherhood of man at all times, consciously disavowing the sins of the past by not letting them return to our consciousness, by not permitting ourselves the luxury of indulging in sorrow for them after this moment. When the moment of repentance is over, we are done with them: we are living in the now of our new birth.

The new birth will not last, however, if we continue the habit of looking back. Lot's wife left her old selfhood, turned around to look back at it, and perhaps missed it for a little while, and thereby lived to regret it. But we must close the door of memory on the past, on the old man with his sins of omission and commission, and continue to live in the new birth, the I-ness of now, the nowness of our new Selfhood, the Selfhood that is living the life of love. It does not speak of love; it does not say, "I love you"; it lives in action the life of love.

Making the Life of Love a Continuing Experience

With our eyes closed, let us look out from our withinness and behold this new universe, this universe from which we do not expect to draw anything except what we contribute to it. We express love not only to our friends, relatives, and close associates, but we take the entire world of men and women into this consciousness with us. We have placed love in our consciousness; we have placed love in the world; and that love will flow back to us. But we take no thought for the love flowing back to us; we let it flow as one of the added things. We live in a continuous state of now expressing love.

The love that we express today must become a continuing experience, a love that we express through forgiveness, understanding, sharing. Every opportunity to express love that is presented to us we must accept, and not ask, "Where is it going to come from?" not ask, "How can I do it?" but remember the pattern of our life, which is now based on the truth that of ourselves we can do nothing.

> I drop my burden at the feet of the Christ,
> the spirit of God within me, and all will be
> accomplished by that spirit of God. Whatever it is
> that I am called upon to do of a physical nature,
> of a mental or financial nature, I can do because
> my capacity is not limited to me. I have dropped
> my burden at the feet of the Christ within.

Thus we drop anxiety, the burden of fear, worry, and concern, and live by recognition of the great truth:

> *I* within me is my bread, meat, wine, and water.
> *I* am the Source of my inspiration. *I*—this is the
> Father within me, the Christ within me. I relax and
> rest in the assurance of an inner kingdom that meets
> the needs of my outer world. I am fed from within;
> I am supported from within; I receive my inspiration
> from within because I have learned that I live now
> and not by might or by power, but by listening,
> thereby being attuned to the inner kingdom.

Maintaining Our Awareness

God's grace can reach us only as we are attuned to the kingdom of God within. As God reaches out to us extending His grace, and we are not there listening in attunement or in at-one-ment, then we are not receiving the grace that is ours.

The prodigal son ran away from his father: the father never ran away from the son. We, in our ignorance, have become prodigals by running away from God, but God has never run away from us. The kingdom of God announced by the Master as being within us is still there where it has always been. It was there two thousand years ago. "Before Abraham was,"[7] the kingdom of God was established within us, but when we began to worship through rituals, rites, and other external forms of worship, we turned away from listening to the Father within and living by virtue of Its presence.

An hour from now it may be difficult to remember that we must have a moment to recognize: "I live from the withinness." Three hours from now it may be difficult to remember that we have accepted all mankind as our brothers, and certainly it may be difficult to awaken tomorrow morning and remember that we have already forgiven everybody and that we cannot wake up with resentment, anger, or thoughts of revenge. So it is that there may be a process of forgetting and then remembering, remembering and probably forgetting, and then remembering again. Even though making this conscious remembering a part of every day's activities, it very likely will not be twenty-four hours before thoughts of anxiety, concern, or fear come to us because of the outer circumstances of life. It is not unnatural that for a moment we may forget our resolve to live life now, but to restore ourselves to the rhythm of God, we remember as quickly as we can:

I have dropped my burden at His feet; I have
acknowledged that there is a Presence within me

greater than any problem in the
external world. I have agreed to find my food within,
to be inspired from within, taught from within,
and supported from within.

I live a life of inner attunement,
so that I may forever be at-one with my Source,
and thereby be at-one with every son and daughter
of God throughout this entire universe.

Breaking Attachment to the Outer World

To those dwelling "in the secret place of the most High,"[8] none of the evils of this world will come nigh their dwelling place. To have a measure of that immunity, let us dwell now in the secret place which is within us and look to this withinness for our good. Let us begin as rapidly as possible to break the attachment to the outside world that says, "Oh, I get my supply here," or "This one owes me something." This does not mean that we change our outer mode of living, but inwardly we break that attachment by the constant realization:

I am fed from within. There is a wellspring
of water within me. All is within me:
the bread, the meat, the wine of life.

It takes a few months, even years, to break this attachment to the outer world, to break the belief that we are dependent on man for justice, for loans, for forgiveness, or for our support, but we can do it if we can remember the word *now:*

Now I and the Father are one. Now do I
draw upon the kingdom of God within me.
Now do I seek living waters within myself,
the bread of life, the staff of life within myself.

No longer do we seek from "man, whose breath is in his nostrils,"[9] but now we know that our attunement to the withinness of our being is the secret of the spiritual life, turning within a hundred times a day just for a momentary remembrance: "Thank You, Father. The kingdom is within me"; a hundred times a day, just smiling at the remembrance that now we are one with the Infinite. The entire Infinite is flowing forth into our experience.

This turning within must go on and on, this conscious remembrance of deriving our good and our protection from within. Whatever it is that appears in life as a problem, the answer is instantly to turn within, realizing that the solution is within us. Then we relax and go about our business, but keep up the practice throughout the day and throughout the night.

As the months go by, a new experience comes into our lives. One day we will be conscious of the fact that we have received some kind of a message, an assurance, a direction, or a command from within. It may be startling at first; we may even wonder if it is really true and may even lose the benefit of it by not realizing the real nature of it. All of this makes no difference. We have before us an eternity, and as we continue this practice, it will happen again. We will have a direct awareness of some response from within, or something will happen to our outer life that we will recognize could not have happened unless there were an invisible transcendental Something bringing it about.

This is really the beginning of the spiritual experience for which we have been preparing through all these months of living now, living consciously in the realization of now; but at some particular point we receive our first impartation or blessing, which we recognize as coming from within. Let us be patient. Let us not think that now that this has happened it is going to be a completely permanent, continuing experience, because it is not. But the fruitage of the realized Presence will be apparent more and more frequently.

God Prays in Us

All this is leading to the place where we can consciously relax our remembering, because we have attained a place where we are so completely in attunement that the praying comes to us from within. Now we will come to the higher unfoldment of the Infinite Way, to a place where we no longer pray, where our prayers do not take on any measure of thinking or speaking: it is God that does the praying in us and through us, and we merely become aware of the activity of God that is taking place within. We are then always on the hearing end; we are always on the receptive end, the receiving end. God is praying in us and through us. This is the meaning of "Man shall not live by bread alone, but by every word that proceedeth out of the mouth of God."[10]

In the first stage of our spiritual life, the one I have been describing to you, we maintain the word of God in our consciousness; we constantly remember and declare the word of God, and even send it forth. As we come to the second stage, however, the word of God comes forth from the kingdom within us, and we receive it; we do not speak it or think it: we hear it or feel it. It is all a flowing from the within to the without. By that time we have so completely reversed our life that the whole experience is one of inner attunement, an inner flow from the within to the without. But there must be these preceding months in which we prime the pump.

Now

The great word is *now;* the important word is *now:*

> Now I have forgotten my past; now I have surren-
> dered my past; now I am living in the new birth.
> Now I and the Father are one. Now I live by the
> grace of God—not by might or by power.

Now I have laid down my burdens at His feet, and I
let the spirit of God within me maintain, sustain, and
feed me. Now! Now that I have laid down my wor-
ries, my anxieties, my fears, I let the still small voice
instruct me. Now I come to the Father, not to tell
Him the despairs of this world or of my world, for He
is not there. Now I come only to listen and receive
divine Grace. Now I have dropped these burdens.

Now, Father, where Thou art, I am; where I am,
Thou art, for we are one. Here in this withinness we
are one; and I am one, spiritually, not only with the
Father, but with the sons and daughters of God, universally. Now I am of the household of God, and I
have taken all the sons and daughters of God into my
heart, into my spiritual household, and I share with
them. I express love in deeds, not in words, but in
deeds, in acts. I am living the language of love.

Love is my relationship to God; love is my
relationship to the children of God. We are
united in the inner kingdom, in his Presence,
all receiving His grace. We are dependent, not on
each other, but on His grace that is within us.

Could you not watch with me one hour? Could you not
pray for the sons and daughters of God all over the world?
Could you not daily remember that you have been ordained to
comfort, to heal, to lift up, to forgive, to bless, to open your
heart that His spirit may flow forth now?

Limited Love Gives Way to Universal Love

In one of these moments of spiritual communion, we will
feel a great love for every man, every woman, and every child

who is on the spiritual path. It will not be a limiting love; it will not be a love felt only for those on our particular spiritual path: it will be a love that will embrace everyone, worldwide. Regardless of the name or nature of the teaching each one follows, we will feel that love, because we will feel a great oneness and will know that the same longing to be united with the Father that is within us is within them. This will be the first experience of a worldwide love that comes into our heart, and it is this that makes it possible to look out at all the rest of mankind and say, "Father, forgive them; for they know not what they do."[11] Then we let that love draw them in as well.

The first and the easiest step is to look around to those on our particular spiritual path and feel a love for them, knowing that all of us are working toward the same goal: a conscious realization of the Presence within. Then our vision goes further, and we realize how many more throughout the globe are longing to know God aright, waking early in the morning to meditate and unite with God, staying up late at night, and getting up in the middle of the night to unite with Him. So our love flows from nation to nation, worldwide, taking in every praying person, every person who is living the life of prayer and meditation.

With that comes the discovery that there is only one spiritual path, and that is the path of God-realization, although it may take many, many forms. This then opens the way for that further love of compassion: "Neither do I condemn them, their sins be forgiven them."

Being an Instrument for God's Grace to the World

The entire responsibility rests upon us. It is we who are recognizing the now; it is we who are loving our neighbor as ourselves; it is we who are abiding "in the secret place of the most High"; it is we who are living in the Word and letting the Word live in us. So it is eventually we who attain that inner communion, that inner at-one-ment that lives forever after by a spiritual grace. Without our consciously entering upon this path, without our consciously abiding in these moment-by-moment realizations, the ultimate success could not come to us, that ultimate experience of His grace.

Every day, at least once, inwardly let us raise our hands, as if we were holding them over the whole world and letting God's grace flow through us to this world. We are doing nothing of our own account: we are letting ourselves be the instrument. It is as if these hands were up over the globe, and from these hands went forth God's grace and God's blessing to all who are receptive and responsive. In the secrecy or privacy of our own room, we can even do it physically and have the feeling of the love of God flowing through us, but otherwise we can do it silently, the same way as we meditate, just silently, inwardly lifting our hands, letting them cover the globe, and then letting the spirit of God flow, always remembering that what we put out into consciousness is what comes back to us as the added things of this experience.

Always we carry with us these two passages which will be very important in our spiritual life. First, "My kingdom is not of this world"[12]: the spiritual kingdom, the Christ-kingdom, is really within us. Whatever we want of the Christ, we seek within ourselves. Then having established that within us, come these words, as if coming up from within: "My peace I give unto you."[13] The Christ-peace, the spiritual peace, the peace of the Father is given unto us. Always, every day, let us feel that peace welling up from within: "*My* peace, the spiritual peace, God's grace, give I unto the world."

ACROSS THE DESK

Nothing can ever be accomplished tomorrow. Whatever is done can be done only in the now.

So, too, is it with the life of the Spirit. The goal of attunement to that Spirit within is never attained by hoping or wishing for it, promising that tomorrow more time will be set aside for meditation and the deep things of the Spirit. We can begin only now—never tomorrow.

Now, in this moment stop to listen, keeping your ear open for inner guidance and instruction. This practice of pausing frequently without any words or thoughts in an attitude of listening is opening yourself to the flow of the Spirit within until life is lived in a continuous state of conscious awareness of the omnipresent activity of God. To do this thirty or forth times a day would not be too often. The time required is less than a minute each time, but the rewards in spiritual awareness are very great.

Do not resolve to do this at the beginning of this New Year or tomorrow, but do it—and do it now! Fulfillment be yours this New Year.

TAPE RECORDED EXCERPTS
Prepared by the Editor

Nothing can be more important to our spiritual progress and to the peace of our daily experience than living in the nowness of Being. These brief excerpts will help to focus your attention on this important principle.

Living in the Nowness of This Moment

"Wake up every morning and open yourself to God. Let God fulfill Himself in you today. God may go as far as to let you know what to do tomorrow and next week, and if so, do it. But do not let your thought go further than that. . . If you would live in this minute, agreeing that the power of God is functioning in you, and let that continue minute by minute, you will find no concern about the past and very little about the future, and in one way or another you would know day by day what to do, and sometimes for weeks in advance."

Joel S. Goldsmith, "Spiritual Healing Continued,"
The 1957 Chicago Open Class.

"While our watches are marked off with little periods called seconds, minutes, and hours, if we remove the watches and clocks from the world, are there any marks anywhere in this universe indicating a past or a future, or are we not always living in the consciousness of now? Of course, there is no such thing as a mark anywhere that reveals a past or a future. Life can be lived only in the now. Then whatever life you are living in the now is the only life that you possess. . . ."

Joel S. Goldsmith, "The Spiritual Sowing and Reaping Now,"
The 1962 Glendale Open Class.

Chapter Two

The Spiritual Goal

On the spiritual path, we have a definite goal, a specific place to reach. That goal is not the gaining of good health, better morals, more abundant supply, satisfying companionship, or a beautiful home. These are the added things that come with the attainment of the goal. If we had these other things and did not attain our real goal, we would still have nothing but baubles and bangles, nothing but shadows. When we have attained our goal, we have all the added things as the fruitage, including permanent harmony, permanent peace, permanent health, and permanent abundance.

The Experience, Not Words

The first step is reaching the awareness of the presence of God. It is not the final one: it is the first one. We may intellectually agree that God is omnipresence, that the kingdom of God is within us, or that Christ dwells within us. This can in no way be considered the attainment of the goal. That is merely making a statement about it, merely affirming something that we hope eventually to experience. Our goal, however, is not the declaration and not the intellectual knowledge that there is an indwelling Christ: our goal is the actual experience of the Christ.

We can talk about food forever and starve; we can talk about water forever and thirst. We must have the experience of eating and drinking in order to be satisfied. So talking about truth, voicing truth, or hearing messages of truth may be very well in its place, but it is not a very satisfactory place. We begin to know satisfaction only when we experience the Christ. Then we, too, can echo Paul's statement: "I can do all things through Christ which strengtheneth me."[1]

The ultimate goal is conscious union with God, but that goal is reached by comparatively few persons. Regardless of the efforts they may make, they are, for the most part, preparing themselves for that ultimate experience in some future life. There have not been many in the recorded history of the world who have attained actual conscious union with God.

Every Individual Is Free in the Infinite Way

The letter of truth serves as a guide or bridge for us to travel over, but the letter of truth itself is not sufficient to take us into the kingdom of God. There must be the actual experience or consciousness of the Spirit before we reach that goal. It is for this reason, then, that we use what we know of the letter of truth to help us gain our end. On this particular path, that of the Infinite Way, we devote a great deal of time and attention to meditation, because it has been my experience and the experience of those whom I have taught that for us meditation is the best way of attaining our goal. There is no one way ever discovered that may be called the right way for everyone, and probably there is no way that may be called the best way; but the way of meditation is our way, and it is best for us.

Some who come to the message of the Infinite Way do not remain with it, and it is for this reason that we continue to be unorganized and without memberships, so that students may come and students may go in accord with their own spiritual light. There is never any tie binding anyone except the invisible tie of mutual interest, love, and help. Each student is free to study, to meditate, to unite with us in our spiritual activities, and at any time that he discovers that this is not his way, he can leave with blessings, with love, and with the same degree of friendship that we had while we were working together because no ties have been broken. The only tie there ever was, was a spiritual tie, and that will never be broken because we are calling no man on earth our father. My Father is your Father, and your Father is my Father; we are brothers and sisters, regardless of what particular religion or spiritual path we may follow or if we follow no path at all.

Ask Not for Anything of This World

Our first step in meditation is the contemplative meditation where we ponder some scriptural passage. We have all had the experience of trying to meditate and finding that our thoughts wander all over the city and country, and because of that experience it became clear to me that if at first we take some metaphysical, mystical, or scriptural truth into our consciousness to ponder, it is easier to hold our attention to the truth.

Let us take the passage, "My kingdom is not of this world."[2] The very first thing that comes to my thought as I make that statement is: If the Christ-kingdom has nothing to do with this world, there is no use in my going to the Christ-kingdom for supply, companionship, an automobile, a home, or employment. I had better park those desires outside. At first that may shock the student. I am sure it shocked me many years ago, because I had always looked on God as someone to whom we went for our earthly requirements. But right off I am told, "My kingdom is not of this world."

Then I remember that Jesus did say, "Take no thought for your life, what ye shall eat; neither for the body, what ye shall put on."[3] That is right. I am not to go into prayer for food, clothing, or housing; I am not to go into prayer for anything concerning the material life.

This biblical passage brought forth the following statement in one of our classes: "You can go to God for anything you want, as long as it is not anything of this world." That may sound limiting or restrictive but it will give us a very large field. We can go to God for love, understanding, truth, immortality, peace, but not the peace that the world gives. "My peace I give unto you: not as the world giveth,"[4] not the kind of peace that can be gained by having quantities of money, abundant health, or a beautiful home. No, "My peace," the Christ-peace, the Christ-kingdom is made up of something entirely different from any earthly good, any earthly peace, or any earthly harmony. So we are reminded at the very beginning that we are not to go to God for anything of an earthly nature.

Receiving Instruction from Within

Since we cannot know what the kingdom of God is, it must be revealed within. We must be instructed in the ways of God from within; we must be instructed in the nature of the kingdom of God and the Christ-peace, and we can be instructed only by God because so far no man has ever written anywhere, not even in scripture, what the kingdom of God is like. If anyone has known what the kingdom of God is like, he has never been able to write about it or tell about it. To discover that we must go to Headquarters and be taught of God.

"Speak, Lord; for thy servant heareth." [5] Thou art
closer to me than breathing, nearer than my own
hands. Speak to me; reveal Thyself to me.

At this point of meditation, our speech and our pondering come to an end, and we are all ears now, inwardly listening for that "still small voice." [6] We may not hear anything audibly, and in the beginning we may receive no impressions inwardly, but this is of no importance, because the Spirit has begun Its work in us. At the very moment when we are still and open our consciousness to receive God, at that moment God consciously enters. After that, we may not come face to face with God for many years, but there is never any possibility of coming face to face with God unless we take this first step.

Sometime or other there must be the first step of opening consciousness to the presence of God. Until then we are not on the spiritual path, even if we have read a thousand books. It is not in the reading of books that we gain wisdom: it is in the opening of our soul-faculties, of our spiritual faculties—these must be opened. The Master referred to these spiritual faculties when he said, "Having eyes, see ye not? and having ears, hear ye not?"[7] He was not speaking of our physical eyes or physical ears, He was speaking of those inner faculties, and these we must develop. The development begins with the very first time that we consciously take the attitude of "Speak, Lord. I am listening for Thy voice. Instruct me!"

As we persist in this experience of opening consciousness to the presence of God, eventually we do get an answer. It may not necessarily be an audible answer at first, although sometimes it is. There are no formulas in the spiritual life; no two people have the same experience. It may be our good fortune to hear that still small voice, or even a loud thundering voice, with our first experience, or it may not be so. Again, it is not important, regardless of how it may be. The only important thing is that we have opened our consciousness to receive the presence of God, the spirit of God, or the Son of God, call It by whatever name you will.

Ripeness

As we continue to abide in meditation and turn within for the realization of the Presence, a ripening process takes place.

This term is not a familiar one with most Westerners, but in the Orient a developed spiritual person is called ripe. Being ripe means having attained this inner spiritual consciousness and the ability actually to commune with the Spirit within. That is a ripe soul. In China it is called an old soul. An old soul is one so matured in Spirit that he actually is in the Presence and has the ability to tabernacle or commune with the inner Spirit. It must be noted, however, that there are many wearing robes who are not ripe, and the wearing of the robe does not constitute being ripe.

The ripening process begins with our first turning to truth, even before we learn about meditation. From the moment we opened our first book of truth, our consciousness was beginning to change, leading us step by step. Through following one teaching, we may have been led all the way or we may have been led from one teaching to another. The Spirit works in us and leads us to our good by a way that we know not of.

Our Motive Is the Ripener

Many times students become discouraged because after a certain number of years they feel they have not made the hoped for progress. If it is any consolation to those who may be discouraged with the apparent slowness of their progress, they should understand that it is very unusual to feel any progress until one second after awakening. We cannot feel it coming on; we cannot know even one minute before that we are on our way to spiritual awakening. As a matter of fact, we may continue in sickness or in sin even while we are making the most remarkable spiritual progress, ready for our illumination, and yet with no evidence of that readiness, wondering when the moment does come, "How could it happen? Five minutes ago I was in deep sin, and this minute I am an angel."

It makes no difference if we take the wrong path, we will end up where we belong if our motive is right. We need not be concerned whether the particular message we are following is the highest or the best. Our concern should be with our motive. If that motive is to know God, then we can be in any teaching or no teaching and still be assured that we are going to end up knowing God aright, because the ripener of our soul is our desire or motive. When the heart cries out to know God, to tabernacle and commune with God, when the heart pushes us forward, compels us to read, listen, or study, when something within is driving us, be assured we are ripening, even though at the moment our outer experience does not bear testimony to it.

We go through years of suffering, either in illness, in lack, or in actual sin, and then, "in such an hour as ye think not the Son of man cometh,"[8] and we are awake. In every case where I have seen this happen, the answer has been the same. Deep down there was a longing to know God aright, to know truth, a longing to find the nature of "My kingdom," or the nature of "My peace," and as we continue in our study and meditation, regardless of whether we feel spiritual or not, the ripening process is going on.

Discount Any Feeling of Spirituality

As a matter of fact, if we feel too spiritual we should be a little bit suspicious of ourselves, because it is not natural to feel spiritual. There is a good reason for that, just as there is a reason it is unhealthy to feel honest. Heaven help the person who thinks he is honest, because we all have the right then to question it. The person of integrity does not go around feeling honest; the moral person has no feeling of what it is like to be moral. If asked what it is like to be moral, he cannot tell how he feels about it.

So it is with the spiritual nature. I do not know that there is any particular feeling that might be called spiritual. At times there are emotions that arise, although I question very much if they are really spiritual emotions. Instead, let us learn to disregard what we think of as our feelings and be concerned only with the fact that our motives are pure, that we are continuing to study, continuing to meditate, and eventually we are going to break through.

Seek God for God

There are certain principles that help us to hasten the day of our spiritual awakening. When we go into meditation, the first principle to remember is that we are not going to God for anything, unless it be that God speak to us. We are not going to God for health, wealth, companionship, or a home. We make sure that we are not going to God for any motive because this is the barrier to God-realization, the almost insurmountable barrier. To do that would be like thinking of God as a way station to what we wish to attain, and that would make God our servant. "Dear God, go out and get it for me," implying that there must be something more important than God.

But there is nothing more important than God. If we attain God-realization, everything will be added unto us in abundance. All good things are added; every phase of divine harmony is added; and most of these are made tangible in what we call our practical world. It is literally true that in the attainment of God-realization most of the problems of this world disappear.

It really requires deep sincerity to be able to go to God with this attitude:

> I give You my word of honor,
> I am not coming to You for anything except You,
> Yourself. I am not looking beyond You to what You
> can do for me, or what You can get for me.
> In fact, I am willing to renounce all that. Just let me
> come into Your presence; just let me know Your
> grace; just let me tabernacle and commune with You.

At first this is difficult because even if we do not think of ourselves, the temptation is to think of our child or grandchild, and we want to reach God for him. In that desire, we have set up a barrier. Or we may have a patient and hope to use God to benefit the patient: "Really, God, I know it is unselfish, because I do not want You for me, but for this dear soul I am helping." That, too, is a barrier. We must go to God completely pure, completely humble, completely ready to relinquish this world.

The Master used other words for it, but he meant the same thing. He made clear that we must leave all and follow the Christ. When we go to God, we leave all of this world, give up all our friends and relatives, and go to God only for communion, only for oneness, only for the joy of being in the presence of God, and then leave all the rest to God. All the *things* will be added unto us, and those in our consciousness requiring healing will also receive healing in proportion to their own openness to the spiritual Presence and Power.

Freedom in the Realized Presence of God

In our work we have found it helpful never to want God-power for anything. Otherwise a conflict is set up, and this conflict is a barrier. In the kingdom of God there are no evil powers. In metaphysics it is said that sin is not a power, disease is not a power, lack is not a power, evil is not a power. Of course that is only a half truth. They are very much power in the three-dimensional world. In fact, the whole third dimensional world is suffering from those very powers. Therefore, it does not help very much to engage in these denials. The truth is that in God's presence they are not powers. The truth is that where the spirit of the Lord is, there is freedom. That has nothing to do with being free in this world, or having health or a lack of evil powers.

This whole world is made up of evil powers, far more of evil than of good powers. It is only when we attain God's presence that we can say that evil is not a power, that it is not even here.

It is only when we are in the presence of the Lord that we know we are free, because there is no bondage in the presence of the Lord. Where the spirit of the Lord is, there is freedom, freedom in spiritual perfection, not freedom from anything for there is nothing to be freed from once we attain the presence of God. So our whole function on the path of the Infinite Way is to attain the realization of the presence of God.

A person may say, and rightly so, "God is omnipresence," but I will add, and also rightly, "So what?" What good is it to those who are in slavery? What good is it to those who are living in totalitarian countries? What good is it to those who are suffering from some form of bondage? Omnipresence is a power of divine harmony only where omnipresence is realized. God is the liberator only where God is experienced. God is the healer only where God is realized.

No Power Is Needed

Where there is even a tiny bit of God-realization, an individual begins to do healing work. Where this God-realization is of a deeper nature, he does better healing work. If it is possible that we may again have a Jesus Christ on earth, we will probably all have instantaneous healings. But it will be the same God and the same people; the difference will be in the individual who has attained that height of God-realization.

If we work, study, and meditate from the standpoint of not using God as a power, not trying to get God to do something for us, for our patient, or for our child or grandchild, just being willing to relax in the Spirit, it will be easier to rest in the power of the Word. As we *let* the spirit of God be upon us, we will be ordained to heal the sick, to comfort, to bless, to increase the loaves and the fishes; but there must be this *letting* of the spirit of God be upon us. We make no mental effort; we do not think of God as a power, for in truth, God is not a power. God cannot be a power, because there is nothing for God to be a power over or upon. God is being, pure being, and besides God there are no powers for God to act upon.

God may be described as the one and only power or as the non-power. Personally, I have had the greatest fruitage in my life when I have been able to sit quietly with a sense of God as non-power, as Being, just pure, omnipresent Being, and not seeking for God to do something to the errors of this world. In that state of consciousness, the errors that confronted me melted.

No Mental Struggle in Isness

So, too, it is a help in attaining God-realization not to be struggling mentally to get to that point. After all, the place that we are seeking to attain, we already are. We are right now at the place of our goal; we are now in the presence of God. Neither life nor death can separate us from God, nor can sin or purity. Therefore, we are already at the place which is our goal, although we are not yet aware of it. We are not going to go any place, up or down: we are merely going to awaken inside to the realization that the place whereon we stand is holy ground.

> Right here where I am, in a room or on a battlefield,
> any place where I am, is holy ground, for
> "I and my Father are one."[9] Neither life nor death
> can separate me from the love of God, the life of
> God, the presence of God, or the power of God.
> The place I am going is where I already am.
> Therefore, I need no powers. I do not even need
> God-power to get me there: I am already there.

It is said that no one runs after a trolley car when he is on it, and I am saying that we do not have to mentalize to reach God, because we are there.

"Be still, and know that I am God."[10] In quietness

> and in confidence you receive your peace,
> the peace that passes understanding, My peace,
> spiritual peace, the kind the world cannot give.
> It comes in quietness, not mentalizing, not
> declarations—in quietness. Be still! Be still!—Let the
> robe descend upon you; let My grace envelop you.

There are no powers to act as a barrier unless we permit the desire for something other than God to intrude into our consciousness, and then we set up an internal warfare. But as long as we are pure in our motives we will attain.

> To know Thee, this is my goal.
> I can do without food; I can do without clothing;
> I can get along very well on very little. Let me not
> take thought for those things. Just let me be still.

Once we have stopped going to God for something that is beyond God, that we want God to get for us, once the goal is God Himself, once we have seen that we do not need a God-power to do something to something or someone, we are so close to the kingdom of God that it will be a miracle if we do not fall overboard and find ourselves drowning in it. So close are we to the kingdom of God that we attain it the moment we lose our desires, the moment we stop thinking of God as a power, the moment we stop thinking of God as a means to some other end. This is how close we are to God. The only barrier is a mental obstruction, the idea that God is a power that can do things, or the idea that God is something that can go out and get something for us, send something, or give something.

Good Is Already Omnipresent

We cry to God for supply, and we forget that the earth is filled with gold, silver, platinum, oil, and all the other treasures.

We keep praying to God for supply, when all the fruit trees are filled with fruit. God cannot add supply to us, and really all we are doing when we pray for supply is saying, "God, address it to my residence." God has already filled this earth with more supply than all of us who are on the earth will ever use. It is folly to pray for more supply; there is more here now than we need. The storehouses are full of it; it is rotting in the barns. Supply is ample, but God is not going to address it to our residence. There is no supply except God.

"I am the bread of life." [11]
Once you attain the realization of Me,
you have your bread, and your meat, and your wine,
and your water, for *I*, God, am these,
and when you have Me, God, you have all these.

We pray to God for life eternal, as if God and life eternal were two separate things, "God, give us more life!" God *is* life, and it is only when we get God that we have life eternal. Again it is given to us in the words of the Master: "I am come that they might have life, and that they might have it more abundantly."[12] *I* is the secret. In getting the realization of *I,* the realization of this presence of God that is within us, we have life, and we have a life more abundant. But we will have it only in first having God.

It is folly to believe that there is God *and* supply; it is folly to believe that we can pray to God for life. Pray to God for God, and you have life eternal. Seek only God! Leave mother, father, brother, sister; leave your human sense of life and enter into life eternal. Surrender this false sense of life and watch how the life of God envelops you.

As long as there is the grace of God, the presence of God realized in meditation, the life of God acting as a constant renewal, then this very life on earth is a joyous experience. But in traveling the world I know that it is so only to those who have attained even a drop of God-realization, but to the others life is still a burden.

Pondering Truth and Then Listening

Instead of long periods of meditation, we should have as many periods of meditation in the day and night as possible. Those who are beginning to meditate usually find that three times a day is about as much as they can manage, considering all the rest of their human duties. After a year, some of those human duties do not seem so necessary, and they will have been discarded, making way for six or seven periods of meditation. By the time a person meditates for a few years, he will discover as we have, that he can eliminate many of those human obligations and spend twenty or thirty times a day in meditation and still not neglect his family.

In meditation, after we have come to the end of our pondering, there should be one or two minutes in which we sit in a listening attitude. I never recommend more than one or two minutes, not until students are far along in meditation because for young students it is not possible to hold a silent meditation beyond a minute or two. The mind begins to wander, and then it is no longer meditation. It is only meditation in those brief seconds when we are still and listening. The minute thoughts begin to percolate, the meditation is over. Only one second of complete silence would be enough. That lets the Spirit in and lets It function!

There is no room in this work for falling asleep during meditation or for mental stagnation. Meditation is a very vital activity; it keeps us alive and alert because in the beginning we are pondering a specific facet of truth, and we are marshaling together all the arguments for it that we can from scripture or from metaphysical writings. By the time we settle down to listening, we are really alert, waiting for that "still small voice." Sometimes it is so still it will go right by us if we ourselves are not still.

To know Thee aright is life eternal. Let this be our goal, to know that Thee within us, and let all the rest be added unto us.

Across the Desk

Some students in their enthusiasm want to rush out and give the Infinite Way message to their world before they have let it become established and solidified in their own consciousness, forgetting that no one has anything to give anyone except as the fruitage of his attained state of consciousness. They are unwilling to wait for that and often lose the pearl they have been given, either through personal ambition for place and power, or through gross ignorance by prematurely attempting to give out what they have not yet attained and what has not become their own realized consciousness.

It is a principle of the Infinite Way that consciousness draws to itself its own. Therefore, the students' all-important consideration must be the development and unfoldment of their own consciousness. The way of that unfoldment is clearly given in the Infinite Way: study of the letter of truth which sets forth the principles, meditation, and the moment by moment and day by day practice of these specific principles.

With such a program, diligently followed, students will be building a solid foundation. The light of their consciousness, obscured by lifetimes of humanhood, will be shining so brightly that it will be a beacon drawing those who can respond to that light.

No real Infinite Way student ever seeks any outer spiritual activity or seeks to draw anyone to him. His only concern is that his own consciousness unfold. That consciousness will reveal itself as whatever is to be the form of his spiritual service, but he will not *seek* it. His work is to be still and behold God in action.

Tape Recorded Excerpts
Prepared by the Editor

As this month's letter and the following excerpts from the tape recordings indicate, there is no way of measuring how far or how close we are to the goal. But we can know that we are approaching it if we live each moment doing the work of that moment, meditating, and living out from whatever degree of spiritual light has been given us.

Measuring Spiritual Progress

"You read in the religious literature of the world how many there are who are continuously fooling themselves that they are experiencing the Presence, people who are having nothing more nor less than an emotional jag. The religious literature is filled with accounts of people who are victims of self-hypnosis, who write the most fantastic things and experiences. The way we know that it is not a true spiritual experience is that there is no practical fruitage from it: there is no peace attained; there is no harmony attained, no health. None of the experiences that have come to the world through the revelation of Jesus Christ come to those who live on cloud nine and do not keep their feet on the ground.

"The experience, when it is attained, immediately acts to set one free. Free of what? First of all, concern. That is the first fruitage of the attainment of the Christ. . . Problems may linger for quite a while, or problems may come and problems may go. Some problems may be solved through the activity of the Christ, yet other problems come to take their place. But this is the normal, natural experience of life until, through the continued realization of spiritual identity and spiritual life and law, one may come to the place described by the Master, 'I have overcome the world.' But let us not believe that he uttered those words in the first month of his ministry."

Joel S. Goldsmith, "Daily Preparation for Beginning and Advanced Students,"
The 1961 Waikiki Infinite Way Study Center.

"For centuries, we have lived in a sense of separation from God . . . whereas the revelation of all the mystics has been oneness. This is very difficult to believe because there is no time in your life when you ever feel that you are God, or when you ever feel that you are spiritual. You may have a few moments of emotion, ecstasy, or seeming to be on cloud nine, but there will always be an hour from then, or tomorrow, and that sense of separation breaks in because you can say to yourself, 'I cannot be one with God because I feel human. Probably, I even have a physical pain or a financial lack, and if I were one with God, this could not be.' . . .

"You must not judge by the appearances of today, nor must you try to judge your progress, because no one on the spiritual path can ever evaluate his own progress. Actually what happens is that we go along, sometimes for years, feeling that we are making absolutely no progress. Every mystic has discovered that he meditated, he studied, he practiced, he did whatever he was instructed to do, in spite of not seeming to make much progress, and then all of a sudden, one minute of one day, or one second of one night, 'Whereas before I was blind, now I see,' and the 'old man' was dead, and the new man was born."

Joel S. Goldsmith, "Consciously Attaining the Experience of Oneness," *The 1963 Kailua Private Class.*

Chapter Three

Becoming Aware of God's
Ceaseless Activity

This latter half of the twentieth century is perhaps the first time in recorded history that so many persons in the Western world have been seriously interested in a mystical message. When I say "so many," do not understand me to say that I mean great numbers, but I do mean that for a message of this nature the number is large. There are probably sixty thousand homes in the world in which the Infinite Way is read, but in those homes probably only ten thousand students earnestly study it. How many there are who actually practice it is something I have no way of knowing. Those who are serious in their study will bring forth a fulfilled experience in their lives, and their number is sufficient to make a real contribution to the world.

What determines the nature and the extent of our contribution to the world, however, depends on the extent of our own individual demonstration. For many years I had absolutely no interest in any "you" anywhere in the world, none whatsoever. I had only one interest in life, and that was discovering the secret of why God is not in the human universe, how He could be brought into it, and more especially how He might be a part of my experience. My interest in the world was purely academic;

there was no thought that this work would actually help the world. My goal was to seek God for myself, to see if God could be brought into my personal experience.

First Attain the
God-Experience Yourself

I was living the same kind of a human life that nearly everyone else lives on earth, and even with some of its successes, it was not satisfactory. In fact, with a considerable measure of success, there remained an irresistible drive to find out if God could be brought into my experience so that something of a different nature could take place. What that would be, I had no way of knowing. Therefore, my experience for years and years had nothing to do with the world: it had to do with my seeking, my searching, and my goal. It was only after the spiritual experience came to me that my life began to be lived out for the world, and then not because I would choose it that way, but because it was an impelling thing from within.

Every student must make up his mind that until he actually attains the God-experience he should not think in terms of benefitting or blessing the world, because spiritually he has nothing with which to bless it. He may be able to contribute financially to worthy causes; he may be able to contribute inventions or discoveries through his inventive capacity, but spiritually he has no contribution to make until he has had some measure of the God-experience, that is, until his life shows forth some measure of spiritual fruitage.

Therefore, study, meditation, contemplation, and communion must take place within the student until he receives the signal to go further. To bring this about or to deepen and enrich it in the experience of those who have had it, there must be a prolonged period of study, meditation, communion, and contemplation until the flow from within begins and becomes evident without.

I and the Father Are One

What we in the message of the Infinite Way are now trying to demonstrate is first of all the truth that "I and my Father are one."[1] When the meaning of that revelation first came to me, I thought I was the only person who knew it and probably the only one who had discovered it. Since then, however, I have acquired a large library, and I can assure you that there is nothing that I have ever said or am going to say that is an original revelation. When Jesus Christ said, "I and my Father are one," that was not original even with him. Five hundred years before, Buddha taught that there is only one Ego, one Self, one Life, and *I* am that. And long before that, this same truth was revealed through Krishna and others. As a matter of fact, centuries before Jesus, Moses revealed that there is only One: "I Am That I Am."[2] So while there is nothing original about any discovery, there is something original about the mode of its presentation and its practice, and that is what we are dealing with in the Infinite Way.

"I and my Father are one" is the revelation, the promise, the conclusion, and it is that which you and I are to show forth in our daily living. We are not to hug it to ourselves; we are to share it with all those who seek it.

The Spiritual Meat and Bread

To bring this truth of oneness forth from intellectual knowledge to realization, let us contemplate that truth with our eyes closed and the world shut out from us:

> "I and my Father are one." All that the Father has is
> mine. I am alone inside my own being, and at the
> moment not even aware that there is Another within
> me, that inner, greater part of my Self.

"I and my Father are one," but the Father is greater
than I. At this moment I am aware only of me,
myself: I am not aware of the greater part of my Self,
the Father within. This is the invisible part of my
Self; this is the Storehouse of my good, and it is
This with which I am seeking conscious union.

"I have meat to eat that ye know not of."[3]
What is that meat? How should I use that word
meat? Is it not a spiritual word signifying Grace?
Does it not mean that I have the power of Grace
within me: security, safety, peace,
the source of health, the source of abundance,
the source of love? Does it not mean that
I have within me what the world cannot see and,
therefore, cannot deprive me of?
I have the source of intelligence, the source
of wisdom, the source of love.

I have within me the source of
the cement of human relationships—love—
the source of life, the source of harmony,
the source of peace, the source of understanding.

This is what we mean by *meat,* spiritual meat.
The Master also used the word *bread.* "I am the bread of
life."[4] So we can use the word *bread* in the same way that we use
the word *meat:* food. "Man shall not live by bread alone, but by
every word that proceedeth out of the mouth of God."[5] This
gives us a whole new meaning:

I have the word of God within me that the world
knows not of. I have within me the Word, the Bread,
the Source, the Good, the Substance of life.

We are not referring to anything of a material nature. It is all spiritual. The meat, the bread, the word—these are all spiritual, the source of our outer supply of peace, safety, health, joy, abundance, sharing, companionships, friendships, family. We have the source of these, the substance of them, and the world knows it not, but we *have* It.

The Have-ness of Being

Let us think for a minute of the word *have*. Most of us, at one time or another, have made an effort to get something either through God, through metaphysics, or through treatment, and now we can see why it was inevitable that we failed. Since "I and my Father are one," and all that the Father has is ours, there is nothing left for us to get. "I *have* meat"; and "I *am* the bread." Every time we have looked to God, to truth, to prayer, or to treatment for something, we have set up the very barrier that has kept it from us because we embody and embrace within ourselves all that the Father has; it is ours.

What does the Father have? What is the Father? The Source, the Substance, the creative Principle of all that is, and all that is embodied within our very being.

I have meat the world knows not of:
I am the bread of life; and this Source has come
that I might have life and that I might have it more
abundantly. It is established as my very identity.

Here where I am, within me, is the source
of all I may ever hope for, long for, desire, or need.
All this is established within me because
it is my Father's good pleasure to give me
the kingdom. When? Not tomorrow! Now!
God can do nothing tomorrow!
All that God is, God is now.

The Law of God Operates Now As Fulfillment

Even the law that causes the sun to rise tomorrow is a law of God that is operating now. If it were not for the nowness of the operation of the law of God, the sun could not rise tomorrow, for God could not start tomorrow to make it rise. If it were not that the law of God is now operating, the seeds that are in the ground now, which are to become fruits and vegetables months from now, or flowers, could not appear in their season.

There is no God to operate in the future; the operation of God is in the now, even though the fruitage may appear in its season. Some trees blossom in spring and summer and some bear fruit in the fall. All this is in God's season, but it is because of the nowness of God. God does not make the snow to fall in the wintertime: it is the operation of God throughout the year that produces snow in its due season.

Regardless of the fruitage that is to appear in our lives tomorrow, next week, next month, next year, the law that sets it in motion is our knowing the truth of God's nowness and withinness. We must know the truth that the source of our supply of love, life, health, harmony, wholeness, protection, safety, and security is not outside of us: it is within us, but it is our recognition of this truth that produces it in the without in God's season.

We must not look at any temporary barrenness and from that judge our lacks or limitations. We must look at this barrenness with the understanding that God's law is operating within us: "I am come that they might have life, and that they might have it more abundantly."[6] Then, in its due season, in place of the appearance of barrenness there will be fulfillment.

There is no real barrenness. For example, if we should look at a coconut tree after it has been stripped of its coconuts, we would judge it to be barren. But there is no barrenness there. In the withiness of that tree, the process is now taking place that will produce more coconuts in due season. "Judge not according to the appearance."[7]

In any period of lack or limitation in any facet of our experience, let us realize that this is not a time of barrenness, but a time for the realization of the operation of God, the continuity of God's grace, the is-ness of God, and the withinness of God.

What is taking place in my consciousness
at this moment—my realization of the withinness
of God's grace, God's law, the withinness of
the source of all that is—is the assurance of
some form of good to appear in my outer experience
today, tonight, tomorrow, next week, next year.
I am bearing witness that now within me
the grace of God is functioning because I and the
Father are one; all that the Father has is mine; and it
is His pleasure to give me the kingdom. Therefore,
the Father's spiritual love is fulfilling me; His spiritual
grace is guiding and directing me; His spiritual grace
is the meat, the wine, and the water within me.

Listening Receptivity

Mystically, dwelling on spiritual truth is living a life of prayer and contemplation. It is as if we were priming the pump by these reminders of truth. Then, with this understanding established in us, each day we come to the second part of the contemplative life: communing with the Spirit within us in which we stop all thought and listen.

We can begin this listening period with half a second or a full second of silence. That is sufficient because if we have enough of these periods and come to this moment of listening, even though it lasts only half a second, we find that eventually, of its own accord, it will stretch itself out into a second, two seconds, three seconds, and ultimately a whole minute. No one needs any more than that.

There will be occasions when, for some special reason, we

may be able to maintain that listening attitude for minutes and minutes and minutes, but that is because God has made it possible for us to relax for that length of time in order to be receptive to whatever it is that God is imparting to us. Usually, however, anyone who can be still and listen for one minute and can repeat this at will as many times a day as he wishes, will find that he has been fulfilled and that his life begins to take on an entirely different nature.

Spirit Takes Us Beyond Human Good

This does not mean that from the time we begin to meditate our life is going to take on the nature of sitting on cloud nine and that everything is going to be harmony, peace, and love. I would be misleading you if I gave you any such promise or assurance. The Master, himself, did not hesitate to say, "Think not that I am come to send peace on earth: I came not to send peace, but a sword."[8] By this he meant that eventually we are not going to know or experience *human* good at all. Our good is to be of a spiritual nature, an entirely different nature from just having a doubled income, a perfect heart, or even a perfect body.

In the beginning of our spiritual experience, it is true that our health improves as well as our sense of supply. It is not always that our income increases: it is that much of the money that has been spent for unnecessary, foolish, or wasteful things is no longer spent that way, and there is, therefore, more money available for the necessary and important things of human experience. In other words, less of our money goes into waste products, and more of it into the good things.

We do experience improved health, improved supply, and in some ways, improved human relationships. But it is also true that we lose a great many of our friends and some of the members of our family. We cannot expect that because God has opened us to this way of life, it will open them to it also. If they will not be opened to it, gradually there will be a falling away, and that is a period, for many people, that is very unpleasant. Humanly we love our friends and we love our relatives, but when our way of life is no longer their way of life, there does come a separation. We have to be willing to leave mother, brother, sister, father for this purpose. It does not mean to desert them, but it does make a difference in our relationships.

Our Divine Inheritance

In our human world it is believed that we began with our mother and father, and because of that belief, we have lost the whole secret of the Master's teaching: "Call no man your father upon the earth: for one is your Father, which is in heaven."[9] There is but one Parent, the Creator, the creative Principle of us, that which is responsible for us. It may even have been responsible for the coming together of our mother and father, but above all things, we know God is responsible for our being here. Therefore, God has planted the seed of Himself within us. We call this the Christ, or we call it the *I* of us, the Self of us.

Through the Infinite Way I have learned that the greatest word of all is *consciousness*. Unless I am conscious of these truths, they do not manifest. Unless I am consciously aware of the truth of being, unless I consciously abide in God and God in me, unless I consciously hear the still, small voice, unless I consciously subject myself to the law of God and the will of God, I am just another member of the human race. To be just another member of the human race is not enough: we have a divine heritage, a spiritual heritage; we are the children of God. "Know ye not that ye are the temple of God, and that the Spirit of God dwelleth in you?"[10] Our consciousness really is God, and when we are in meditation we are receptive and responsive to the presence and the power of God that becomes the activity of our consciousness.

This spiritual life is not a lazy life. It is an active and a joyous one when we have really learned to live a life of contemplation and meditation. For a time this may bring disturbing influences into our experience; it may even bring up latent illnesses in our body; but that may give us the opportunity of experiencing a spiritual healing, and thereby purify the body, with no latent diseases or signs of age to come forth. All of this, however, has to be done consciously. There is no other way.

God Is Working Out Its Plan in Us

Humanly we have built up ideas as to how our supply should come or where we would like to live or what we would like to do. But once the spirit of God begins to take hold of us, It begins to work out Its plan in us. It does not work to fulfill our plan or our desires, and if anyone thinks that God's purpose is to serve our human will, he will soon learn, through this work, that that is not true. God is not meant to fulfill our human desires: man was created to show forth God's will, God's plan, God's life.

The human race is not doing this; that is why it is at war with itself. It is set on fulfilling its own desires, its own will, its own way, and of course there is no grace of God in that experience to bring it to fruition. Spiritual fruition can come only as we surrender our will and our desires.

> God's will be done in me. I am not trying to tell God
> how I want my life lived, or what I want God to do.
> I am submitting myself in meditation to God's will,
> God's way, God's plan, that I may be an instrument
> through which God's plan on earth may be fulfilled.

Furthermore, if that means eventually giving up our business, that is the way it has to be. If that means eventually living in some other place, that is the way it has to be. We are not going to move and we are not going to give up anything: we are submitting ourselves to God to let God move us as God will.

We were not placed on earth for any reason other than to be instruments through which God's grace, God's will, and God's plan might be fulfilled on earth. Humanly we are not doing this. It is for this reason that we are now on the spiritual path on the way to our return to the Father's house. We have been prodigals with a will of our own, a desire of our own, a hope of our own, and we are now returning to our Father's house. "Nevertheless not my will, but thine, be done."[11]

The Grace of God Realized in Meditation Is a Law of Multiplication

"The earth is the Lord's, and the fulness thereof,"[12] and "Son. . . all that I have is thine,"[13] ours for sharing, for we are all children of the one Father. We are all brothers in Christ, of the household of God, and what belongs to one belongs to all of us, not through any communistic system of division, but through the spiritual system of multiplication. There is no need to divide. The Master taught us the law of spiritual multiplication, not division. He brought forth multiplication of the loaves and fishes, and so do we. We share, but not from any idea of believing that what is humanly thine is mine, but from the spiritual grace of love. Through love we share with each other, but only because we know the law of multiplication that never ends.

Close your eyes and see that within you is this kingdom of God. Within your consciousness is the activity of the grace of God functioning twenty-four hours a day, three hundred sixty-five days a year. The grace of God is functioning within you to renew, to multiply, to rebuild even "the years that the locust hath eaten."[14] But do not look outside of you; look within and realize:

Here, within me, within my very own consciousness,
the grace of God is operating
to fulfill God's abundance,
to fulfill the infinity of God in me and

through me, that I may take
the twelve baskets full and share them.

Here within me now is the law of God,
the grace of God which is to appear as coconuts on
my tree next month, as flowers on my bushes,
as birds singing in my garden,
as twelve baskets full of substance and
supply for me to share with my neighbors,
with those who have not yet realized that the law of
multiplication is at work within them, not outside.

The law of multiplication is working within you and within me, here and now and forever. Our contemplation of this truth is what sets it in motion and keeps it in motion, as long as we are obedient so that when it appears, we share.

At Christmastime, our household is filled with mail from all parts of the world, with love, greetings, and gratitude in every possible form. But, if I did not immediately place that on the throne of God and then share it, it would dam itself up. No more could come in, and no more would go out. As I have freely received of love, joy, gratitude, and grace, so must I share with the world through the tape recordings, classes, and in other forms.

The main point to remember is that it is in our periods of daily contemplation of these truths that this law which has been operating in us since "before Abraham was"[15] is enabled to come forth into expression. The world lost it through having lost the practice of silent prayer, meditation, communion, and contemplation. If we live constantly out here in "this world,"[16] we set up a sense of separation from the Source, because the Source is within us, that "meat" the world knows not of. We have an infinity of meat and bread and wine and water, but it can come into manifestation only through an activity of consciousness. What does not take place in our consciousness will never take place in our world. If we do not have love for God and man in our consciousness, thereby fulfilling the two Commandments, we will not find God's love or man's love flowing to us. First it must be an activity of our consciousness before it can flow from us and to us.

Restoration and Renewal Through Contemplation and Meditation

To abide in the Word and let the Word abide in us is meditation; this is contemplation; this is communion. What Word? "If a man abide not in me. . ."[17] That *Me* is *I:*

> "I have the meat to eat that ye know not of."
> I have within me the meat, the wine, the water.
> I have within me the power of resurrection,
> and if you destroy this temple—
> whether it is my health, my body, my home,
> my family, my anything—if you destroy any
> of these temples, my conscious oneness with
> the spirit of God within me, attained
> through contemplation, will raise it up again.

Job lost everything and tried all the known ways in the Hebrew religion to have all the things he held most dear restored, and they were not. In the end he discovered the secret. Whatever has been lost or ever may be lost out of our experience, the way to resurrect it is the way of contemplation and communion. That is the message of the Master, more especially as revealed in the Gospel of John, the message that refers to the *I* that is within, the Father within, to that He that is greater than any personal sense of "I."

We are like the iceberg: one-third of us shows above, and two-thirds is hidden beneath. So it is that when we look in the mirror, we see only the one-third of us, at best, a limited concept of the two-thirds that is invisible. The two-thirds of us that is hidden is the Father within, the *I* that in reality we are, the *I* that has come that we may have life, and that we may have it more abundantly.

When we see the barren soil or the barren trees or the barren bushes, we can smile to ourselves as we think of the law of nature that operates in the trees and the plants. "No, I know better. There is a law operating within that in due season will bring fruitage to the without." If we can do that, we will have the clue to this entire subject of contemplation and meditation. If we can look behind the universe and see that a spiritual law, an invisible and incorporeal law, is operating and appearing outwardly as the movement of the earth, the planets, the stars, the sun, the moon, the tides; if we can see that all this that is in the visible world is functioned by the Invisible, we will begin to perceive the nature of the contemplative life, the fruitfulness of the life that is lived in prayer, meditation, and realization.

As we witness those things, we understand the message of Jesus Christ: "Greater is he that is in you, than he that is in the world.[18] . . . The Father that dwelleth in me, he doeth the works.[19]. . . I can of mine own self do nothing."[20] From that message it is clear that the way is meditation, communion, living, moving, and having our being in the realization of our inner Self, which is the great two-thirds of us, the source of the other third, without which there would be no other third.

ACROSS THE DESK

Many students do not realize the importance of developing the healing consciousness. Long before they have even begun to develop this consciousness they yearn to have an Infinite Way activity or even to teach. There may be a vague feeling that the healing consciousness is reserved only for the few who become actively engaged in the healing work, which may account for the fact that so few students make a really serious effort in this direction. But the Infinite Way was never meant to be simply another teaching, the inner mysteries of which only a few could comprehend and make practicable in their experience.

The Infinite Way is a way of life, a most practical way, which carries with it the command, "Go thou and do likewise!" Everyone must live the Way in his daily experience by meeting the problems that arise by the practice of the Presence and the recognition of the problem as the appearance of a life or being separate and apart from the One. If every situation were faced in this way, gradually such a consciousness of oneness would be built that each and every student would be showing it forth in his daily life.

While our goal is the attainment of God-realization, there is no better way to reach that goal than through this practice. If the Infinite Way is something that is going to help our soul unfold and we think of that as separate and apart from life, then we are a divided household. But the Infinite Way is a healing ministry in which each one of us must be involved. Those students who seek to become more active in Infinite Way activity can begin this moment by doing healing work and thereby developing their consciousness.

TAPE RECORDED EXCERPTS
Prepared by the Editor

The next several Tape Recorded Excerpts will point out tape recordings and give excerpts from them which set forth clearly the basic principles of spiritual healing and living so that students can work with these excerpts and the tapes, if they have access to them, and thereby take a big step forward in attaining the healing consciousness.

One of the most important principles of spiritual healing is an understanding of the nature of God as "of too pure eyes to behold iniquity," a God so pure that to It evil is wholly unknown and has no existence, a God of pure Being. This principle, which makes it possible to relax in the is-ness of God with confidence and assurance, will certainly take on new meaning and have greater relevancy in your experience if you will contemplate and live out from the idea presented in the following excerpts:

God As Pure Being

"As you have looked out upon this universe and witnessed the divine order of the sun, the moon, the stars, and the tides, as you have witnessed the divine order in apple trees giving apples and rosebushes giving roses, as you have witnessed the divine order in the rotation of the seasons, you have to acknowledge that there is a Cause that operates through law and that certainly operates through love.

"This alone will bring a tremendous release within yourself once you have acknowledged that this universe has a creative Principle, a Cause, Something that sent it into expression and form and Something that maintains that expression. This relieves you, individually, of all responsibility. It enables you to relax and realize that that which sent you into expression must likewise be that which maintains and sustains you and all mankind.

"Once this is acknowledged, you have set yourself free of all concepts of God and you have merely acknowledged that God is, and that God is that which functions through law, through love, that which functions as a creative Principle, a maintaining and sustaining Principle, and then you can rest in that. You can rest assured that that which is maintaining the integrity of all nature can maintain the integrity of your and my individual life."

Joel S. Goldsmith, "God, Prayer, Grace." *The 1960 New York Open Class.*

"There is no way to 'love the Lord thy God' except one way, and that is to understand fully and to become convinced within that evil has no foundation in God, that evil does not have its rise in God, that neither sin, disease, accident, death, famine, storms, nor drought—none of these comes from God. Only in the degree that you can remove the foundation of evil can you become free of it, and it has its foundation in the theological belief that God, in some way, is responsible for it. . .

"To ascribe evil in any form to God is to make God lower than man, for of man it is demanded, 'Be ye therefore perfect.' We would never consider any man perfect who visited sins and diseases and death on other men—not for any reason. Even in this modern day, mankind is developing enough love, enough understanding of the spiritual nature, that he is even doing away with the death penalty for those who commit murder. Now if man is that just and that considerate and that knowing, think of God! Could God demand death of you or of me for any reason, when we are that righteous that we no longer believe in death, even for murderers?. . .

"If we can do that, how much more does God do? How much more of love, intelligence, life, and of purity is there in God? To ascribe evil to God is sinful; it is blasphemy. Most of the evils from which we suffer have their foundation in a universal belief that God visits those evils upon us, either to punish us for something, to teach us a lesson, or for some other reason. . .

"The foundation of the evils that beset us are in the universal belief that God is responsible for them, and you and I are ignorantly and unconsciously suffering from accepting that belief. We may never have consciously thought of it, but nevertheless, because it is in consciousness we suffer from it.

"To begin to set yourself free from the penalties of these universal beliefs, you must set God free of all responsibility for the sins, the diseases, the deaths, the droughts, the lacks, and limitations of this world. You must begin to honor thy Father which is in heaven. You must begin to love the Lord thy God with all thy heart and with all thy soul, and love Him in the realization: 'Thou art of too pure eyes than to behold iniquity or to cause it. Thou art the very light of the world, and in Thee is no darkness at all.' Then, when you have a God wholly good, you have yourself wholly good, for 'I and my Father are one.' . . ."

Joel S. Goldsmith, "Two Steps to Spiritual Freedom,"
The 1961 Maui Class.

Chapter Four

We Cannot Solve a Problem
on the Level of the Problem

The spiritual life is dedicated to the realization of God as the source, the cause of life, and even the effect itself. It is also a revelation of immortality. Immortality, however, does not mean longevity. In fact, longevity and immortality have no relationship whatsoever to each other. Longevity has to do with a little longer span of physical or human life, whereas immortality has to do with the complete circle of life, that is, pre-existence before you came to this plane, and your experience on this plane, as well as the completed circle of life which goes on after this human span and relates more to the life of the Spirit than to the physical sense of life.

If you are to understand immortality—and you must understand it if you would enjoy health, harmony, vitality, and youth of mind and body—you must understand that it relates to your immortal life, the life that has no beginning, as well as the life that has no ending. You cannot think of immortality as merely the continuity of this life after death.

Life Without Beginning and Without End

To understand immortality means to understand the scriptural statement, "In the beginning God. . . ."[1]—in the beginning life, in the beginning your life—"God created man in his own image, in the image of God created he him."[2] All creation has reference to the beginning, to God's own life as It is manifest or shown forth as the Son: God the Father and God the Son as one. Therefore, if you think of God as having no beginning and no ending, you must necessarily think of life as having no beginning and no ending, and if there is but one God, there is but one life. That one life, therefore, must be yours and mine, and it must be an immortal and eternal life.

When you come to the teaching of the Master, you have it stated very clearly: "I am come that they might have life, and that they might have it more abundantly.[3] . . . Before Abraham was, I am."[4] As a matter of fact, "I am with you alway, even unto the end of the world"[5] that you might have life, life before Abraham was and life unto the end of the world.

"The end of the world" does not mean the world as we know it coming to an end. It means the coming to an end of that state of limitation within you which measures life by time. Actually time has no effect upon life. Life is external to time. Time is only a measurement that is used. For instance, as you look up at the clock, you can readily see that it has no relationship to God, God's universe, God's world, or God's time. You yourself have set those hands so that they read a certain hour. Just across the ocean it is a different time. This is all a man-made arrangement. It is only a convenience that the clock is arranged into a twenty-four hour period for work, rest, study, for purposes of communication, and so that industry can operate on an orderly basis. Take that clock away, however, and you will discover that there is no such thing as time: there is only the movement of the planets and the rotation of the earth on its axis which is measured by hours and minutes.

Once you remove the clock and the calendar—and both of these are man-made—you no longer bring yourself under the bondage of time, and you can better understand the Master

when he says, "Before Abraham was, I am. . . I am with you
alway, even unto the end of the world." In those two statements
you have the entire circle of your life: "Before Abraham was"
and "unto the end of the world." Within that circle you experience birth and within that circle you experience the passing on
that has erroneously been called death; but within that same circle there is also rebirth, and then another death. There are continuous birthings and dyings until you break through this limitation of human sense and gain an awareness of your own life as
eternal. "I am come that they might have life, and that they
might have it more abundantly," at least have the awareness of
it. But even when you are not aware of it you have that life eternal, that abundant life. Now, however, you must come into the
awareness of it because of the effect of that awareness upon your
body, mind, and health.

Have You Overcome
the Fear of Death?

Behind all the evil in this world is the fear of death. Death
is the final and ultimate fear. The only fear that attaches itself to
a cold or to the flu is the fear of death; otherwise you would
ignore it and it would quickly disappear.

You, yourself, must answer the question: Have you overcome the fear of death within yourself, or are you able to ignore
it because you are not yet near threescore years and ten? It is very
simple to have no fear of death when you are thirty or forty, but
you will notice that people begin to think more seriously about
this subject after they pass the threescore mark, realizing threescore and ten cannot be far ahead. So the question that each one
must ask himself is: Have I overcome the fear of death? That
does not mean that you believe that you are going to go on living on this earth forever. It means that you have overcome the
fear of death, even though inevitably you are going to pass from
human sight.

The experience of God reveals the immortality of life, and after that there never is a question of fear. What possible thing can an individual fear who has God, God Almighty, God, the Infinite, the Omnipotent, Omnipresent, Omniscient? Could anyone then fear any experience either of life or of death? "For I am persuaded, that neither death, nor life, nor angels, nor principalities, nor powers, nor things present, nor things to come, nor height, nor depth, nor any other creature, shall be able to separate us from the love of God."[6]

If you cannot be separated from God, from the care, the mind, the love, and the life of God, what difference does it make to you on which continent you are on or which side of the veil, or whether up in an airplane, on a ship, or driving a car on the highway? What difference can it make where you are or what the circumstances are if you have caught this vision of omnipresence?

By acknowledging life and death, you accept what most persons are hiding from within themselves, that inevitably there is a time of passing from human sight. Unfortunately, this time of passing from human sight is called death, and therefore has all the fears attached to it that are attached to the unknown, the mysterious. This all disappears when it is understood that if you, at this moment, are in the presence of God, if at any moment in your experience you have been in the presence of God, that is all there is to life or death, for this experience continues through life and through what the world calls death.

Actually there is no such thing as death. Passing from sight is a transition that takes place normally and naturally at some point in time. With the correct spiritual understanding and light, passing from sight is a normal, natural process, but when the transition is made through disease or accident, it is just a premature experience, one that nevertheless is not death, but only a passing from glory to glory, from one experience to another, from one unfoldment to another.

Drop the Problem

In the very earliest days of my practice, I was given this statement: "You cannot meet a problem on the level of the problem." I would like you to memorize that particular statement. You cannot meet a problem on the level of the problem, and this applies to accident, disease, or death.

Assume now that I am saying to you, "I have a headache. Please give me help." You are about to give me that help, and the first thing that I ask of you is, "Do not think of me or my headache, because if you think of me and my headache, you will perpetuate the headache. As long as you are holding the headache in your mind, you will hold it in manifestation, because mind and manifestation are one, and you cannot separate them."

As long as you hold a thing in mind, you have it. If you are going to hold me and my headache in mind, you are going to immortalize both the mortal and the headache, whereas if you will quickly remember, "You cannot meet a problem on the level of the problem. Joel is my problem, and his headache is another problem, and I must get rid of these before a healing can be brought about. So the best thing for me to do at this moment is to drop Joel and his headache, turn to God, and say, 'Father, since I of my own self can do nothing, you take over.'"

The Inner Release May Come in Many Ways

As you adopt a listening attitude within yourself, the solution to the problem will come. The way in which it comes varies to such an extent that I could not possibly explain all the millions of ways in which it could come. You may, for instance, have absolutely no response within yourself, and it may seem as if you were not being of much help, but you may be assured that if you have instantly remembered that you cannot meet a problem on the level of the problem, you have helped, and the headache is already on the way out. Because you have broken the pattern just by that statement and nothing else, you have broken the continuity, and now neither the individual nor the claim exists in your thought. You have ascended to the Father, and as soon as the pattern is broken, the claim disappears.

On the other hand, it is very possible that the Voice will speak to you and say, "Know ye not, this is My son in whom I am well pleased?" Then you will know that you are being reminded that this is not a mortal coming to you: this is the Son of God. It was only the appearance that seemed to you to be a mortal, and you were fooled by it for the moment. In other words, you were judging by appearances; you were accepting the appearance of a human being and an illness, but now you are gently reminded, "This is my beloved son, in whom I am well pleased."[7] That is telling you that actually what is appearing to you as a human being, a mortal with an illness, really is the immortal life of God, the Father made manifest as the son.

There are other times when as a result of this type of work, there comes just an inner release. You cannot explain it except that Joel and his headache do not any longer bother you. You may wonder, "Have I done enough?" Yes! The moment you have felt that inner release, you are released from the entire obligation.

The answer can come in so many ways, but do not be concerned about the answer. That does not concern you: that concerns the patient. If the patient has turned to you for help, or if someone has turned to you for help for another, more especially for a child or an animal, you can be assured that the help will be received.

Receptivity and Healing

Sometimes you may be called upon to give help to your parents, your brothers, sisters, aunts, uncles, or children who are adults and who are not holding themselves receptive to spiritual healing, and they may not receive the help. That is not because of you. That is because they themselves have the right to open their consciousness to any form of healing they wish or to reject any form. Your concern is mainly with those who are themselves seeking. There is no record in scripture that the Master walked up and down the Holy Land looking for people to heal. He waited for them to come and address him.

When you come to a spiritual teaching of your own volition, not because someone has persuaded you, not because someone has promised that you will get healed, but when something within brings you to this point, you are already receptive and responsive, not only to healing, but to receiving spiritual Grace. You did not do it of yourself: the Spirit already was active in you, leading you in a spiritual direction. Never believe that any human being of his own accord is going to seek the spiritual way of life. It is only if the Spirit is already within him that It compels him to seek books, teachings, or teachers for spiritual light. All persons in the world are seeking health, harmony, peace, or abundance, and therefore if that were all that is necessary, they would all be on the path. They want those things, but not this way. They insist on choosing how they are to have them.

This way is a difficult way. It means surrender; it means a yielding of one's self to something greater than his mind, his wisdom, his education, his ego. It is a yielding to that which the Master described as "the Father that dwelleth in me."[8] "Greater is he that is in you, than he that is in the world."[9] All are not yet ready to lay down the ego and say, "I can of mine own self do nothing,"[10] and then let this Spirit show Itself forth from within.

To Give Help, Climb Into "My Kingdom"

You will remember the Master has given us the passage: "My kingdom is not of this world."[11] Stop just for a moment with that, and go back again to the example of my request for help. With that call you would immediately remember that the Christ-kingdom is not of this world. Therefore you must take no thought for the things of this world or the persons of this world. You are to take no thought about Joel or his headache. Then what are you to take thought for? "My kingdom," the Christ-kingdom, the spiritual kingdom.

> In the spiritual kingdom there are no mortals;
> in the spiritual kingdom there is no disease;
> in the spiritual kingdom there is life eternal,
> immortality, eternality, perfection.

> In the spiritual kingdom no one has ever
> fallen from Grace. In the spiritual kingdom
> man does not live by bread alone, but by every Word
> that proceeds out of the mouth of God. This is the
> kingdom with which I am now concerned.

> In the spiritual kingdom there is a divine harmony,
> God-maintained and God-sustained. In the divine
> kingdom nothing enters that defiles or makes a lie.

After something of this sort has unfolded to you in your contemplative meditation, you can pause for a moment of silence, listening. Again you are able to feel a release; and even if you do not, your work is done, and you are bound to get a report of improvement or healing, because you have not allowed your thought to dwell on this world, but on My kingdom.

The Master promises us, "My peace give I unto you: not as the world giveth, give I unto you."[12] So perhaps this comes to you:

> "My peace," the Christ-peace, that is what flows forth
> through me. I am not to take thought for human
> beings or headaches or any other ills of the flesh or
> pocketbook, because the peace that the Christ gives is
> of a different nature, of a different realm. I am to
> take no thought for this world. I am to take no

> thought for the healing of headaches,
> for "My kingdom is not of this world,"
> and "My peace" has nothing to do with this world.
> I live and have my being in God-consciousness, and
> God knows nothing of human beings or their woes.

If God knew about human beings and their woes, there would be no human beings and no woes because He would take care of them. But the human being and the human being's woes are entirely of what has been called the Adam-dream, mortal existence, an existence and a selfhood separate and apart from God, not a real separation, only a sense of separation from God. When you come back into oneness with God by severing any connection with the problem, you will have lifted the human being up to the status of his true identity.

A spiritual practitioner, looking at a person with his eyes or hearing him with his ears, realizes that an appearance of mortality is being presented to him, but if the practitioner truly has received spiritual enlightenment, he can look through that appearance and realize, "No, what have I to do with thee? I know thee who thou art, the Holy One of Israel, the spiritual offspring of God."

Take Thought for the Kingdom Within

Not only are you to turn from the problem to that inner kingdom, but you are commanded to take no thought for your life, what you will eat, drink, or how you will be clothed. For example, I ask for your help, and immediately you must remember that you are to take no thought for my life or for my health.

What are you to take thought for? Jesus tells you very plainly: "Seek ye the kingdom of God."[13] Then, because you have ignored my life, you will find that the harmony of my being will be added unto me. If I have asked you for help for supply, you must ignore that, too. You must take no thought for what I am to eat, or what I am to drink, or wherewithal I am to be clothed. No thought! No matter how hungry I appear to be or how homeless or how ragged, take no thought for these things, but seek the kingdom of God. Go right back in your consciousness to the kingdom of God. The Son of God has lived since "before Abraham was" and will live unto the end of the world, and always there has been and is Something that is providing for the Son of God.

Do not engage in a battle with lack and limitation; do not do battle with sin; do not become involved in a battle with disease. Rest in the Word! Seek ye the kingdom of God! You cannot seek the kingdom of God anywhere except in your own consciousness. Play with that idea for a few moments. You cannot seek the kingdom of God in a book; you cannot seek the kingdom of God in a holy mountain: you can seek the kingdom of God only in your own consciousness.

Every time that you are called upon for help, you must stop thinking of the patient's life, the patient's health, or the patient's supply, and instantly seek the kingdom of God within your own consciousness. You retire within; you ignore the person and his claim in your meditation. Above all things, never take the name of the patient or the name of the disease into your contemplation. Never, never, never! As quickly as possible, drop all thought of the patient or the problem and seek the kingdom of God within your own consciousness. You are one with the Father, and all that the Father has is yours. This is a universal truth.

> God constitutes individual being. Harmony is the only reality in the kingdom of God. Unto the end of the world, I am maintained and sustained in divine harmony and peace, law and order.

Seek ye the kingdom of God! Stay up there in consciousness with the spiritual truth about God and spiritual man, the spiritual offspring. Never permit your thought to come down to the level of the patient; never permit your thought to come down to the patient's claim. Stay in an uplifted state of consciousness and then if you are lifted into the spiritual atmosphere, you will draw your patient right into the kingdom of God where you are. Very soon you will hear that he is free or on his way to freedom.

Release Those Closest to You

This sounds as if it might be relatively easy, and for a number of people it is. A special group of people find this hard to do, however—parents and grandparents. They have a difficult time because the Master has specifically told them to leave mother, father, sister, brother, and children. Parents and grandparents find that it is much easier to leave some person unrelated to them out of their calculations than it is to leave their children and their grandchildren. That is the Achilles' heel: leave anything but them! Yet, if a person would benefit his children and his grandchildren, in fact if he would benefit all who turn to him for help when he sits down to meditation and healing work, he will have to leave them somewhere outside. He cannot let them enter into his consciousness. If he would really bless them he must leave them out, make believe he can trust God with them, at least for a little while.

Usually it has been found that God really does take care of those children after they have been released to God, but if a person is going to take them or their problems into his consciousness, he is not going to do a good job of spiritual healing. The very ones he wants to help the most, he will end up helping the least, because God is not any more concerned with a person's mortal child than with the person meditating. Therefore, parents will have to raise their children up to their spiritual identity, and the only way they can do that is to drop the children out of their thought. Climb up into that kingdom of God and realize that God has no stepchildren; God has no illegitimate children; God has no sick children; and God has no bad children.

God has only His beloved Son in whom He is well pleased, and this Son is immortal and eternal and universal. This Son is really the life of all individual being. Do not try to bring that person up there. Leave that human identity out here while you are tabernacling with God and with the spiritual offspring of God. Then when you come down from your mountaintop of spiritual vision you will have lifted whoever has reached out to you up into the kingdom of God.

"I, if I be lifted up from the earth, will draw all men unto me."[14] All those who are in my consciousness will be lifted up. That is exactly the way in which I do my work for our classes. Never once do I permit any human person to come into my consciousness. I sit back and embrace the class in my consciousness. How? By ignoring the human beings who will make up the class, and seeking the kingdom of God, seeking the realization of God as the class.

> God constitutes the mind and life of my class.
> God is the very soul of every individual in the class.
> God is the continuity of life, the immortality of life.
> God is the name and the nature of every individual.
> God constitutes the qualities of every student.

> My class is infinite because God is
> the measurement of my class. My class is eternal,
> undying, because God constitutes the life of my class.
> My class is an understanding class because God
> constitutes the mind of every individual of my class,
> and every individual is spiritual.

That is the way you have to pray for the members of your household, your home, your community, your government, and international government. You have to behold God as constituting individual life, individual mind, individual Soul, and not be concerned about the identity, not be concerned with whether they are friends or enemies. As a matter of fact, you have to give much more prayer to your enemies than to your friends.

Release All Thought of Human Peace on Earth to God's Government

You cannot meet a problem on the level of the problem. When you are thinking in terms of world peace, you are not to think of the absence of war, of the overcoming of an enemy, or in terms of victory. You are to think in terms of God's government on earth—not good human government. You might like capitalism better than socialism; somebody else might like socialism better than capitalism; but you in your meditation do not permit your thought to go on to the human scene. You are not asking for human peace on earth, but for God's spiritual government on earth. The only way you will attain that will not be by treating or praying to make bad people good, nor will it be by thinking in terms of victory, but by thinking only in terms of the kingdom of God.

> In the kingdom of God there is but one government,
> and it is spiritual. It is omnipotent: there is no
> opposition to God's government on earth. It is
> omnipresent: there is no place where God's govern-
> ment is not in expression in the kingdom of God. It
> is omniscient: God's government is the government
> of wisdom, intelligence, love. It is omnipotent and
> omnipresent, here where I am; it is there where you
> are, for it is spiritual. It fills all time; it fills all space
> in the kingdom of God. Since the place whereon I
> stand is holy ground, it is here and now that divine
> wisdom functions and divine love governs.

Keep this entire treatment, prayer, or meditation in the realm of God, and do not permit yourself to think of countries, systems of government, or particular rulers or administrations. Keep yourself in the spiritual realm in the same way that you do in taking care of the health of your family, your patients or your students, always remembering that you cannot meet a problem on the level of the problem. If you would remember that statement as you begin your daily period of world work, immediately you would be lifted above thinking in terms of nationalities, denominations, or geographical areas. Your entire treatment, prayer, or meditation would be in the kingdom of God, and soon you would feel a release within that would say to you, "*I* am on the field. My kingdom is on earth as it is in heaven," and the awareness thus attained would be contributing to world peace.

Being an Instrument Through Which God Gives

In the spiritual life there is no such thing as getting. You do not come to a spiritual teaching to get anything, because if you do, you will end being disappointed. There is nothing to get. You come to a spiritual teaching to give, and eventually you will see that there is no other function in the spiritual life than giving. There is no such thing as receiving: there is only giving; there is only being an instrument through which God gives, God expresses, God lives. The moment you think in terms of getting, you are thinking in terms of humanhood, and then you are no longer in the kingdom of God. You are down to this world again, trying to improve it. That has no function in the spiritual life.

Unless you are providing yourself with opportunities for giving and sharing, you are not receiving the benefits of the spiritual life. Giving, sharing, and cooperating have many different meanings. You will, at times, be called upon to share with those who have less than you or who are temporarily in lack. As a matter of fact, it is said, "Ye have the poor always with you,"[15] and I do not think that a student can be on the spiritual path very long before he learns to give something of his income to some impersonal benevolent cause. But the giving that I am speaking of has that in mind only in a very minor way. The giving to which I refer is the spiritual giving, allowing yourself to be an instrument through which you are praying for your enemies and the world's enemies, in which you are praying for spiritual government on earth, realizing spiritual freedom wherever the claim of bondage may appear in any form.

Living in Spiritual Consciousness

The spiritual life is a life of prayer, meditation, and treatment, one in which you are meeting every appearance of discord with spiritual truth, a life in which you are seeking the kingdom of God, and seeking to live there; living, moving, and having your being there; not just returning there for a few moments each day for a prayer or a treatment. The ultimate of the spiritual life is living completely in spiritual consciousness.

The first step is attaining a realization of the truth that each one of us is really two. There is that which appears to be my human identity, which you may call my Joel-hood. That, in its original state, is the "natural man"[16] who is cut off from God, not under the law of God. That is the person who is walking through life subject to sin, disease, lack, limitation, and death. As anyone turns to the spiritual way of living, his first goal is to attain the realization that this is not the full truth about him, that there is a He within that is invisible, a Presence within his consciousness that is invisible. I cannot see it, and you cannot see it. When you look with your physical eyes, you can see only the form. After a while, when you have developed spiritual consciousness, you will behold something else, something far more than the form. It is not visible with the eyes: it is visible only with the Soul-faculties.

As your spiritual consciousness develops, you will be able to look at man, woman, or animal, and behold a spiritual entity, a spiritual light, a spiritual Something that you may not be able to define, but you will know it is there.

Living Out from the Realization of the Christ-Presence

Sometimes students are afraid of the word *duality*, afraid that if they say there is a Christ indwelling, that it means that they, themselves, are not the Christ. It does not mean that. It means that they have a dual sense of themselves, and they need not be ashamed of it. The Master had it too, when he said, "I can of mine own self do nothing. . . If I bear witness of myself my witness is not true."[17] He also knew there was a side of him that was not the immortal Divinity, but he was so conscious of an indwelling Divinity that that humanhood was readily put aside, especially when he could go apart once in a while for forty days to rise above that human sense of self.

In proportion as you are not concerned with gaining victory over disease, gaining victory over enemies, or gaining any victory in life, when you are so lifted up that your whole idea is that the Christ may fulfill Itself, that the Christ may be the leavening influence in human experience, that the Christ indwelling in you be the means of healing, forgiving, and of feeding, do you not see how you have forgotten that *you* want to be fed, or that *you* want to be healed, or that *you* want to be forgiven? You have forgotten yourself, and when you have forgotten yourself sufficiently, you are dead, in the right sense of dying. You must "die daily"[18] to yourself. You must surrender yourself. You must not retain a self that wants to be healed; you must not retain a self that wants to be supplied. You must be dwelling in the Christ which is forever living in you and through you, and which is immortal and eternal.

The longer you think merely of improved humanhood, the longer you delay your spiritual progress. The more you, in your meditation, leave mother, father, brother, sister, and children outside, and dwell in the kingdom of God, the easier it is for you to come back to your normal daily living and find that you are not living with a group of human beings: you are all brothers and sisters, all of one spiritual household, all of the kingdom of God. Everyone who touches your life who is the least bit receptive begins to respond to that spiritual impulse. Then truly it can be said that you live, but not really you: the Christ lives eternally and immortally as you.

Chapter Five

Illumination
through Meditation

The Infinite Way bases its hope for spiritual attainment on the practice of meditation. Without meditation, it is difficult if not almost impossible to make spiritual progress because spiritual attainment is not accomplished through the mind. It is not a mental practice or a mental exercise, nor is it dependent on intellectual proficiency. Rather spiritual attainment has to do with rising above the level of the mind into the fourth dimensional consciousness, Christ-consciousness, or the mind "which was also in Christ Jesus."[1] It is a level of consciousness above that of the reasoning, thinking mind and, in seeking for a way to attain this divine Consciousness, it was revealed to me that the best way lies in meditation. That has been the foundation stone of the Infinite Way since its beginning.

The Illumined Mind, Essential to Spiritual Attainment

On the human level of life it is natural to seek improvement: improvement in supply, health, happiness, safety, and security. Every effort of the human mind is directed to that end: how to be more honest, how to have greater integrity, how to win success, how to win popularity, how to find happiness.

All this can be accomplished through the human mind if a person is willing to devote time and attention to what he is seeking, and even those who wish to attain fame or fortune can attain their goal if they are willing to work hard enough mentally and physically.

But regardless of how hard you might work mentally or physically, you cannot attain spiritual awareness in that way. Paul tells us very clearly that "the natural man receiveth not the things of the Spirit of God. . . because they are spiritually discerned."[2] There is no way for the "natural man" through either mental or physical means to attain spirituality or to bring himself under the law of God. The Master said the same thing when he said, "Having eyes, see ye not? and having ears, hear ye not?"[3] He was speaking of the importance of a faculty or consciousness beyond physical sight and physical hearing. We, too, use certain terms to indicate that there is an area of consciousness beyond the activity of the human mind, words such as the "*still small voice*,"[4] or *the inner ear*.

No life has made this clearer than that of Gautama the Buddha. Despite all his years of seeking, studying, and sacrificing, he accomplished little. But when he gave all that up and sat himself down to meditate, illumination came, that illumination which is spiritual attainment.

Illumination marks the essential difference between the mind of man and the Buddha-mind, meaning the illumined mind, the Christ-mind. "Have that mind in you which was also in Christ Jesus." This is the mind of which the Master could say, "While 'I can of mine own self do nothing,'[5] this illumination, this Father within me, this Christ-mind can do all things." So even if you have not had the experience yourself, you know from these two masters—both on different paths, but who came to the same conclusion—that without the illumined mind there is no spiritual attainment. So the question always remains: How is this spiritual mind attained? How is illumination attained?

By Your Fruits

From some of the Hebrew prophets, as well as from the Master, we know that the way to illumination lies in stillness, quietness, and peace, without taking thought, listening to the still small voice, not thinking, not reasoning, but being still. Gautama gave the world a teaching on meditation which has undoubtedly been lost, because while a great deal of meditation is still being taught or carried on in the name of Buddhism the fruitage is not there. This may be because a form of meditation is being used which is not true meditation, but is just sitting still and not thinking.

Meditation, however, goes far beyond not thinking, and when you study the work of Elijah, Isaiah, some of the other Hebrew prophets, the work of Jesus, John, or Paul, when you read about the work of Bodhisattva and the Zen masters, you become aware of the fruitage in the lives of everyone who really caught the vision. When the fruitage disappears, you may be assured that those purporting to teach a spiritual message have lost the vision.

Seek First the Christ-Mind

To attain through meditation, there must first of all be an agreement within one's self that in the meditation there is no seeking for any thing or condition, but a seeking only for that illumined mind, the Christ-mind, the Buddha-mind, call it what you will—Tao, if you like. Only when you can stop taking thought for your life, stop praying to a Santa-Claus-God with promises to be good if only He will deliver, only when you stop this, will you attain. Stop trying to make God a way station toward gaining your ambition, your hopes, your desires, and realize that there is only one thing that you should desire, and that is that mind that was in Christ Jesus.

At first this may seem to be very abstract. Fortunately, the

Master has promised that if you are obedient, the "things" are added unto you after you have attained illumination. Furthermore, from the experience of every illumined soul of whom there is any written record, you will discover that that person not only was supplied with health, abundance, and twelve baskets full to share, including happiness, peace, and security, but he was enabled to share these with all those who were ready to follow the same path.

"Follow me"[6]: leave all your earthly desires, wishes, hopes, and seek the illumined mind, and all these things will be added unto you. So it has been proved. It has been a most difficult thing for the Western world, because its background of materialism is such that great value is placed on material attainment. If a person has not become successful in his business, if he is a painter and has not gained world recognition, if he is a builder and has not built a Golden Gate Bridge or something equal to it, he is always seeking for that recognition, many times frustrated and disappointed. True, those who accomplish these things gain the world's honors. So ambitious persons have to become president, governor, or senator, and that is not enough. They must gain the office twice, three times, four times, ten times if they can. The world has, up to now, saved its recognition and honors for those of material attainment, and this has resulted in seeking material attainment of itself, rather than seeking first the kingdom of God and then letting the attainment on the material plane be added.

At no time do I discourage anyone from trying to attain health, wealth, or honors, because I believe that the great honors, the high positions, and the great wealth of the world are in the safest hands when they are in the hands of those who seek first the kingdom of God. I do believe that the reward of attaining spiritual illumination should be the attaining of positions of trust, whether in government or industry, because then one is best qualified to carry on the work in the interests of everybody, even of the world itself.

The Activity of the Human Mind Is Not God

All too frequently spiritual attainment is confused with mental attainment. The primitive peoples of Australia, the Polynesians, the Mayans of Central America all engaged in some form of religious practice, and yet not one of these practices is religious in the sense that it has anything to do with God or the spiritual kingdom. Every one of them is an activity of the human mind. The human mind can be used for good or for evil, and that is why there can be good kahunas and bad kahunas, why the primitive people of Australia and those who practice voodoo in Haiti can heal or kill. Any practice that can result in good or evil is not spiritual but purely mental.

"For the law was given by Moses, but grace and truth came by Jesus Christ."[7] That law is both good and evil, and the law can be used for both good and evil. It can be used to reward; it can be used to punish; it can be used to bless one group and also as a means of praying to God to destroy the enemy. That is no different in practice from bad kahunaism or voodooism; it is all cut from the same cloth. When you pray to God to reward someone or pray to God to curse him, it is folly to believe that God is in either of those prayers. It is the human mind, mental law, that can bless or curse.

"Whatsoever a man soweth, that shall he also reap."[8] This has nothing to do with God: it has to do with you and the kind of thoughts you decide you will entertain. "He that soweth to his flesh," that is, sows to wrong or erroneous thinking, "shall of the flesh reap corruption."[9] Again, this has nothing to do with God: this has to do with you and the kind of thoughts you are entertaining.

The Illumined Mind Is a Transparency

Until through meditation you come to that place where you are no longer trying to bless or curse, where you are willing to let God's grace and truth flow through you, so that you are not the actor, the doer, or the thinker, but the transparency through which God's grace flows, you will not have entered that spiritual kingdom, the kingdom of God where you take no thought for your life. You do not do any right thinking for your health, your supply, or your companionship; you do not do any right thinking to bless somebody else. Rather do you become the transparency through which the spirit of God flows, so that you become aware, as the Master did, that of your own self you can do nothing, that it is the Father that dwells in you that does the works. The spirit of God flows through you when you can bring yourself to that place in consciousness where you know, "I can of my own self do nothing, and of my own self I want to do nothing. I want to be still and know that the Father within me, that *I* at the center of my being, is flowing."

When you attain that inner stillness in which you have dropped all desire except that of being a transparency, then you discover that you now have that illumined mind, and it becomes the bread, the meat, the wine, the water; it becomes the law of resurrection; it becomes newness of life; it restores "the years that the locust hath eaten."[10] You do not do it: the illumined mind does it, the mind that you have attained in the stillness of the human mind and which is now a transparency for the Divine.

When we speak of stilling the human mind, we are not speaking of stopping thought: we are speaking of not having a desire, even a good desire, in our thought, not even a desire to help someone. That is being still; that is reaching a state of consciousness from which you can say, "Not my will, but thine, be done."[11] That is real humility. Spiritual humility means recognizing that you have no powers of either good or evil and want none. The only spiritual humility there is, is when you acknowledge, "I can of mine own self do nothing. . . If I bear witness of myself, my witness is not true.[12] . . . The Father that dwelleth in me, he doeth the works,"[13] and then being sufficiently still.

Let me illustrate this point in another way: If I were to have a desire to benefit you and begin thinking toward that end, remember that that same desire or mind that might do this could also turn around the next instant and say, "Well, I think I will be a little selfish in my thought the next time and see how I can do this for me too." In other words, the mind that can do good can do evil.

But if you are to be benefitted spiritually by my work, it has to come about when I am so completely still that I am not even trying to do good for you or bring good to you, when I am so still that the grace of God can reach you and perform Its will in you.

Then afterward, if you say, "Oh, something wonderful happened to me," I can reply, "Yes, by the grace of God"—not, "I did it"; or, "I am responsible for it." No! The most I can ever say is that I am thankful I am a clear enough transparency that the grace of God can operate and perform "the thing that is appointed for me."[14] Therefore, if you were to ask for help on any problem, I must know that there is a He that can perform it, and then I must be very still, so that I do not get in Its way. When the problem has been dissolved and you say, "Thank you," I accept your thanks because I have been a transparency through which it happened, but I do not accept your thanks as if I had done it.

As a matter of fact, there would be no way of my knowing even what is to be done for you. What human being can judge what is good for your tomorrow? None, none! That is usurping the prerogative of omniscience. So remember that your attitude must be that the goal you are seeking is illumination or the Christ-mind. That is your goal! You should have no other goal. You are not seeking health, wealth, position, or anything of a human nature. Your whole goal is attaining illumination. Then, when you have attained it—and even a grain of it is a tremendous power—you will find that that mind will produce the harmonies, the peace, the joy, and the dominion in your experience.

There Is No Power of Evil in God

The idea of using the mind for good and for evil had its origin in the belief that God was both good and evil, that God could bless and God could curse, that God caused life but also that God brought about ultimate death. As long as the belief remains that God can do good and God can do evil, it naturally follows that man will find himself at least trying to equal God and be a power for good sometimes and a power for evil at other times.

Only those who have broken through the level of the human mind and attained even a grain of spiritual illumination realize that in God there is no power of evil, none whatsoever. God cannot bless and God cannot condemn; God cannot give life and God cannot give death; God is always the same, yesterday, today, and forever. There is no beginning to the life of God or the life that God gives, and no ending to it. It is a state of being, but a state of immortal being.

Many students carry with them the ancient superstition of the Old Testament God. Being brought up in a Christian church does not change that because the Christian church adopted the God of wrath, and it has taught, in most instances, that God calls people home in death. Fear and superstition, until recent years, have prevented people from thinking independently. They were afraid to think objectively about religious subjects for fear they would be punished for it. But to some extent that fear has been overcome, and those who have overcome it realize what a horrible thing it would be to believe in a God that struck a person down with cancer or consumption or dropped him out of a falling airplane or let him drown at sea. If there is one idea that is being more widely accepted today than any other aspect of spiritual truth, it is that all of this originates only in the mind of man, which is made up of both good powers and evil powers, good qualities and evil qualities, destructive qualities and constructive qualities.

Illumination Brings a Healing Consciousness

When man breaks through the level of the human mind and catches the first glimpse of the spiritual mind, he will then discover why, when Gautama had his illumination, one of the first things that followed was healing. From one end of India to the other, ashramas sprang up dedicated to spiritual healing. Why? Because the illumined mind always is a healing agency.

Five hundred years later, when the Master attained the Christ-mind, a healing ministry developed. Why? Because the mind of Christ Jesus and the Buddha-mind are the same mind, the illumined mind, and the qualities and capacities are the same. When the illumined mind touches an Oriental or an Occidental, the effect is always the same: it is a healing consciousness, a forgiving consciousness, a consciousness of love. Examine the life of Gautama, follow the life of Jesus, look at the life of John or Paul, and you will find the mind of love, the mind of grace, the mind of peace, the mind of healing. "I am come that they might have life, and that they might have it more abundantly."[15] What is speaking now but the illumined mind?

When an Infinite Way student abandons the idea of trying to use God to gain some human betterment, and seeks only the illumined mind, he will then discover that "ten righteous men"[16] can save a city, a nation, or a world. All that is necessary to perform miracles is to attain that illumined mind.

Desirelessness, a Characteristic of the Illumined Mind

As long as there are desires, you are still in the human mind, because in the mind of illumination there are no desires: there is only fulfillment. There is no lack, so there is nothing to desire: there is only fulfillment. Those who have attained the illumined mind could not possibly have a desire or a need because that mind is fulfillment: "*I* am the bread, the meat, the wine, the water; *I* am the resurrection; *I* am life eternal." In other words, that mind is all of these things; illumination is allness.

The moment you find yourself trapped by desire for anything or any condition, be assured that not only are you in the human mind, but you are going to use human or mental means, unless you pull yourself up quickly and realize, "No, no, no! I am not going to God with a desire. I am going to God for God; I am going to God for illumination; I am going to God for the realization of that mind." Then you will really be on the spiritual path. You will not be at the place of continuing to exchange poor health for good health, and finding later on that it has become poor health again; or exchanging weakness for strength and then, as the years go by, agreeing with the universal belief that when you grow older it is natural to be weak. When you are really on the spiritual path, you will realize that only illumination is important; only that mind, that divine Consciousness, is important. You will live in that realization, letting all these other things be added, because the illumined mind really is the substance of fulfillment at every level of our existence, even on the most practical level.

That mind was practical enough to multiply loaves and fishes for the Master; that mind was practical enough to bring forth manna for Moses, and water, and open out a way through the wilderness for him. That mind was so practical for Elijah that he was fed, even in the wilderness, sometimes by birds bringing food to him. That mind that was in Christ Jesus is the most practical mind there is in all the world. There were miracles of healing, of forgiveness of sin, of supply, of freedom, of peace that came to everyone who touched not only the Master, but many of his disciples and some of the apostles. The most practical way of life that has ever been known is found in attaining that mind.

Resist the Temptation To Change the Human Picture

The way of attainment is through meditation. When you are shutting out the world by closing the eyes, going into the inner sanctuary, into the temple of your own being, you will be tempted. You will be tempted to try to change your health; you will be tempted to try to increase your supply; you will be tempted to want to improve somebody else's health; you will be tempted even to wish evil to some evil doers or to gloat at their downfall, if by chance they have a downfall. But remember, all this is returning to the human status in which there is no permanent good for you. The three temptations that came to Jesus in the wilderness were temptations to improve his humanhood: enhance his reputation, increase his food supply, ensure his protection. Like the Master, you must be able to meet every form of temptation to improve your humanhood with a "Get thee hence, Satan."[17]

Every time the temptation comes to you to change the human picture—and it will come for years and years and years—turn on it. You are going to God; you are going to meditate; and now comes the temptation to see if you can improve your health, your supply, your companionship, your safety, or your security. This you must resist. You have to be steadfast in your insistence: I seek only that mind that was in Christ Jesus, the illumined mind, the awakened mind, the awakened soul. I seek only God's grace. "My grace is sufficient for thee,"[18] therefore I seek nothing but Thy grace.

Every time a temptation comes about some pain, your child's pain, or the bad conduct of your child or your neighbor's child, block it out: "I seek nothing but God's grace. I seek to be a transparency through which God can flow unto everyone and everything within range of my consciousness." Then you will find that you are more or less outside the realm of this world, above and beyond both good and evil, and you will not be measuring out good to some and revenge to others; you will not be praying for the success of one and the failure of another; but rather you will be abiding in the inner sanctuary and letting God govern His universe.

If you cannot trust a God whose name is Omnipresence,

Omnipotence, and Omniscience, then you have no God. You have a concept of God, but you do not have God. When you understand the nature of God, you will be perfectly willing to trust this world to His government, without judging who should be rewarded or who should be condemned.

Wisdom Destroys Unreality

When you have any idea in your mind at all as to who should be rewarded or who should be condemned, you are judging on the basis of the conditioned human mind, and this is not divine wisdom. Divine wisdom does not judge, criticize, or condemn. Divine wisdom automatically destroys that which is spiritually not in line with Its own nature and character. In other words, the wisdom that has made two times two four acts as a law of destruction to two times two is five, and yet without destroying anything because there was no five to be destroyed.

The wisdom that can look out at the sea and not believe in a horizon destroys the horizon, and yet does not destroy anything because there is no horizon. As you go to the desert, if you have enough knowledge so that you can look at any illusion in the desert and keep right on traveling, paying no attention to it, you have destroyed the illusion but you have not destroyed anything. So it is that the mind that is of God destroys everything unlike itself, but it does not destroy any *thing,* only an illusory appearance, something that appears to be but is not.

That is how the Master dealt with the woman taken in adultery and the thief on the cross: he did not judge them; he did not condemn them; he did not criticize them. Why? He left it with God to destroy whatever was not right, but in doing so neither the woman nor the man was destroyed. The only thing that was destroyed was the sin, and it was not a thing. When you take yourself to God, God eliminates everything that is not right, and yet God does not destroy anything, because there is nothing about us that is not right that exists as a thing or as a person.

When the Master seemingly destroyed the fig tree, he was illustrating a principle of the spiritual life. When a person who is indulging human evil seeks forgiveness, repentance, or a turning from the evil, the spirit of God cleanses, purifies, and removes from him not only the evil, but the possibilities of evil and the punishment of evil, so though his sins were scarlet, they are white as snow.[19]

When the Christ touches an individual who wishes to continue in the evil, however, that individual can be destroyed—but not by God. He destroys himself by holding himself up against that presence and power of God and not relinquishing the evil. This is the lesson of the fig tree. Jesus was trying to point out that there was a condition that did not wish to yield itself to the Christ, and therefore the moment the Christ touched it, it was destroyed. So if a person who is evil and wishes to continue in his evil hits up against the spirit of God, the evil will be consumed and the person will be consumed with it. But for a person who, regardless of the nature or degree or depth of his evil, is touched by the Spirit and desires to relinquish it, the evil is consumed and he is made white as snow. While this may appear as though the spirit of God seems to be doing some evil thing in the human experience, it is not really the spirit of God doing it: it is the individual clinging to his evil that is doing it.

You need have no fear of turning within in meditation, whatever the name or nature of the error, because regardless of the fact that you may fall time without number it is not as an actual will or desire. It is only that somehow or other the world's mesmerism is still stronger than your God-realization.

The goal is spiritual attainment; the means, a meditation that does not seek human improvement, a meditation that seeks only an inner stillness and the realization of divine Grace. The law came by Moses—"Thou shalt not." Grace came by taking no thought for your life, but surrendering it in your inner meditation and letting divine Grace be upon you, allowing yourself to be ordained.

Across the Desk

In a previous month's "Across the Desk," it was pointed out that there is great need to develop a healing consciousness and that if you are to be of help to others, they will be led to you. Do not be too eager to begin an activity of the Infinite Way because your own state of realized consciousness will bring to you whatever work you are to do. But for that to happen, there must be that realized consciousness.

Wisdom cautions the student to wait until he is pushed into the work. Then, instead of being overly concerned with saving others, the student must realize that God constitutes individual being and that God is maintaining His spiritual universe.

It is only as you have a conviction and realization that God constitutes individual being that you are practicing the Infinite Way and are able to reinterpret the pictures that are appearing to you as other persons needing help.

Consciousness is the key, so be content to work for spiritual realization for yourself and let the world alone, at least for a little while. Your realized consciousness will draw to you God's work, so devote yourself to attaining that realized consciousness of truth, and then watch the world being brought to your doorstep.

Tape Recorded Excerpts
Prepared by the Editor

To have God as pure Being may not do very much for us if God remains some kind of Being separate and apart from us. There must be the understanding and realization that because of the infinite nature of God, there is room for no other. Therefore, there is not God *and* you or I: there is just God, God appearing *as* individual being. This is a tremendous healing principle with immeasurable ramifications. You would do well to work with this principle in conjunction with the principle of the nature of God as pure Being. Study the following excerpts and attain the consciousness of only One, God appearing *as*.

God As Individual Being

"Our major principle is God expressing Itself as individual being—your being and mine, not your expressing God, not your reflecting God. Never make such a mistake in this work. You are never the doer; you are never the actor: God is forever expressing Itself as the fulfillment of Its own being. God appears as the life of man, woman, child, animal, vegetable, and mineral, regardless of the fact that we falsely entertain a material concept of that life.

"The infinite nature of God means that there can be only one life, and that life is God expressing Itself as life in infinite form and variety or as infinite form and variety.

"With this as your first principle, the very moment a person of an erroneous nature appears to you or any suggestion of an erroneous condition of health, supply, employment, or human relationships, you instantly realize:

> "God expresses Itself as individual Being.
> Regardless of all appearances, regardless of the degree
> of mortality that is presenting itself to my
> eyes and ears, . . . God alone is, and God alone is the
> entity and identity of all being."

Joel S. Goldsmith, "Specific Principles,"
The 1959 San Diego Special Class.

"Every time we are touched with a doubt, a fear, a hesitation, a sense of discouragement, let us acknowledge that what is operating in our consciousness is a sense of separation from God. It is not a separation from God because we can no more be separated from God than this ring can be separated from gold. Why? Because gold is this ring. Gold constitutes this ring, and there is no possible way to remove the gold and still have a ring, because there is not gold *and* a ring. There is a gold ring.

"So it is with us. We cannot be separated from God. Why? Because there is no way. There is no such thing actually in all the world as you or me. God, being infinite, is all there is. God constitutes you and me; God constitutes our being. God constitutes our life, mind, soul, and being, just as much as gold constitutes the ring. Gold is the substance; ring is the form. God is the substance; we individually are the form as which God appears. There can be no separation between us and God. God is the essence of our being, the life, soul, mind, spirit, the law, the continuity, and the activity. God is the all and all of our individual being whether we be saint or sinner.

"The degree of our sainthood is totally dependent upon the degree of our conscious realization of that oneness. The degree of our sinner-capacity is the degree of the sense of separation that is set up within us. . . The moment that sense of separation begins to disappear, Christhood or divine Sonship begins to appear."

Joel S. Goldsmith, "Scriptural Promises Explained,"
The 1955 First Kailua Study Group.

"*As* is one of the most important words in the entire Infinite Way language. God is manifest *as* individual being. . . 'I and my Father are one,' not two. And it is in that oneness that all that God is, I am, since God is the Father and God is the Son. . . God the Father, God the Son, and God the Holy Ghost. . .

"We could explain that in this way God is the invisible you, and the Son is the visible you, yet they are one: the Invisible and the visible. The invisible you is looking out from behind your eyes. . . This that is visible is your form. The invisible you is really the law and the substance of the visible you. . . ."

Joel S. Goldsmith, "The Principle of *As* and *Is,*"
The 1956 First Melbourne, Australia, Closed Class.

Chapter Six

Steps to Union with God

The development of spiritual consciousness is an individual experience. It cannot be brought about in groups. Groups of students gather together, true, but all those in the group cannot develop or grow spiritually at the same rate. Out of every group, there may be one person who becomes a Peter, a Paul, a John, or a Jesus, and there may be a dozen who attain the consciousness of the Seventy or the Two Hundred. But they will not all go forward and attain in the same degree.

No one can progress faster than his own state of consciousness permits, and neither you nor I have any control over that. That is a matter of Grace. One person may devote just as many hours, days, weeks, months, and years to the work as another, as much devotion, as much integrity, and yet not attain one tenth the progress of the other person. There is no criticism, judgment, or condemnation in this. That is simply the way it is.

It has been revealed to me that the secret of all being lies in the word *consciousness*. We are consciousness, not men and women, not human beings, but consciousness. That is our true identity. There are states and stages of consciousness however, and as part of this overall picture, there are certainly states of consciousness in gross spiritual ignorance or spiritual darkness.

Even though there are some persons who believe that God was so displeased with the people of the earth and their disobedience at the time of Noah and his ark that he wiped them all out, enlightened people do not accept that idea, although there are unenlightened people on earth today who live in such a state of spiritual ignorance that they still believe in that kind of God. Never doubt that at some stage of your ongoing and mine, we too believed that. Those who may not believe it in this particular age may have believed it in some previous time, but by now they have outgrown it.

Individual Consciousness Is Evolving Out of Spiritual Ignorance

How great must be the transition in consciousness from the state of ignorance that believed God is responsible for mankind's ills to the state of consciousness where the teaching that God is too pure to behold iniquity is accepted, that God does not hold sinners in condemnation for their sins, or punish them, but that He sent His only begotten Son to earth to teach the forgiveness of sins, the overcoming of sin, and the destruction of sin!

The teaching of Jesus Christ wipes out much of the teaching of the ancient Hebrew scripture, but remember that there are people on this earth today who are still living in the spiritual darkness of ancient times. When you realize that, you will understand why it takes some persons ten years before they can accept truth, and why others may have studied twenty or thirty years and still have made practically no progress. Think of the degree of spiritual darkness out of which some persons have evolved, and are still evolving!

Even the disciples after three years with Jesus Christ were still arguing about whether circumcision was necessary, whether baptism was or was not necessary, or whether the Christ-message was of such a nature that only Jews might receive it. Some disciples became very unpopular with other disciples because they felt that the message should be carried out into the world, beyond the world of the Hebrews, and there was a great strife inside that group.

So it is that you, yourself, cannot be aware of the degree of spiritual darkness or ignorance that was upon your consciousness when you first turned to truth and what layers of that darkness must be penetrated before you are ready to awaken to the significance of the statement that you must "call no man your father upon the earth: for one is your Father, which is in heaven,"[1] thereby wiping out Greek and Jew, bond and free, and making all persons one in spiritual sonship.

Think of the development and the growth that must take place in you before you can look around the world and say, "We are brothers and sisters. We are joint-heirs with Christ in God," and then not put a circle round the Jews, as the disciples did, and claim, "That means us only."

When you undertake this study, you must learn, first of all, not to be impatient with yourself. It is possible that there are long, hard years ahead of you before you awaken to the stature of manhood in Christ Jesus. The Master, himself, said that the way is straight and narrow, and few there be that attain it. And well he knew that, because of the very few who surrounded him. With his great degree of spiritual illumination, not all who came within range of his consciousness were lifted.

To Know What You Are Seeking Is an Advantage

If your progress seems to be more rapid than that of others, there is no reason to be puffed up about it because that also has nothing to do with you. It only means that you have been longer on the path and, therefore, are perhaps better prepared to awaken earlier. It is not you who are responsible for that: it is the grace of God. If you are more quickly or more deeply awakened, then be that much more humble in the realization that you, of your own self, did not do it. It was the grace of the Father, the grace of the Spirit that did it.

You do have an advantage over most of the religious seekers of the world because you know what it is you are seeking. Most persons in the world do not even know what the search for God means and they are still playing around in darkness, not having discovered what the goal is. At least you have discovered the goal, which very simply stated is conscious union with God.

Does that mean that you will never have a headache, a corn, or cramped muscle? Oh, no, because you and I have not yet attained; we have not yet arrived at that place of conscious union. I may have arrived at the place where I intellectually discern that conscious union is the ultimate truth and that that is my ultimate relationship with God. But now I have to prove it. Because you and I, who have been on this path for some time now, have set about to do this, we have attained some measure of that realization. When we attain the complete realization, we will say with the Master, "'I have power to lay [my life] down, and I have power to take it again.'[2] I can walk in and I can walk out, hither and yon, be visible or invisible. I have dominion over every effect, which includes my body."

In some degree, you and I have attained a measure of dominion over the body, over supply, over human relationships. But remember we will not demonstrate the fullness of that until we come into the fullness of the realization of our oneness with God, so that we can say, not intellectually, but demonstrably, "He that seeth me seeth him that sent me,"[3] for "I and my Father are one,"[4] not two: One.

Glimpses of the Goal Do Not Mean Attainment

Do not believe that because you have once had the revelation of what the goal is and have had glimpses of your oneness with God that you will be able to demonstrate it. The demonstration of it comes only by degrees, just as with Saul of Tarsus.

In that moment of blinding light in which he realized the presence of the Christ and was struck by it, he nevertheless understood that the fullness of the realization was not his, and so he did not attempt to teach it until nine years later. Instead he retired into Arabia and hid himself that he might abide with what had revealed itself. That was his new-born Christ, and he could not start out to show forth that Christ in its infancy. He waited for it to be full-grown before he preached and taught it to the world.

So it is that you may have revelations, but do not attempt to teach them until you have retired into the silence for a period, lived with them, and demonstrated them until they have become full-grown in you.

Now that you know the goal that has been given you by revelation, the next point is: How do you attain that goal? How do you span the difference between the human being that you are—the lump of clay, the mortal creature—and that place in consciousness where the spirit of God dwells in you and you are the Son of God? How do you make the transition? How do you do what Paul says, "Die, daily,"⁵ and how are you reborn of the Spirit? How? How?

Ways of Acknowledging God

As part of my illumination, it was given me that the first step is embraced in what is called practicing the presence of God. This means that in any and in every way you should consciously dwell on the idea of God, on some aspect of God, on some spiritual teaching of God. God should be kept in the forefront of your consciousness. Scripture says, "Thou wilt keep him in perfect peace, whose mind is stayed on thee."⁶ Keeping the mind stayed on God is practicing the presence of God.

"In all thy ways acknowledge him."⁷ That is practicing the presence of God. If you awaken in the morning and let your first thought be, "Thank You, Father, for having given us this light of day and for having awakened me to it," you have acknowledged God's presence. If at your breakfast table you pause for a second, even if only to blink your eyes in recognition of the truth that God has set this table—not only when you are next door to a supermarket, not only when you have a pocketful of your earnings, your husband's earnings, or your parents' earnings but even in the wilderness God can set a table—you are practicing the Presence.

If you go about household tasks, marketing, shopping, or business, acknowledging that the presence of God is your wisdom, your strength, and your guidance, you are keeping your mind stayed on God. You are dwelling "in the secret place of the most High."[8]

Noontime provides another opportunity for realizing that your table has not been set by virtue of money or human relationships, but by the grace of God. Thus, throughout your day, your evening, and your night, you find opportunities to acknowledge God's grace, acknowledge His presence and His power, and to acknowledge God's law operating in you and through you and upon you.

Practicing the presence of God is not something you do today and let go of tomorrow. It is something that requires several years of diligent practice. The first six months are so difficult that I know of no one who has succeeded in really doing it consistently, never missing an opportunity. The mesmerism of human life is such that it is easy to forget and then wake up with a start, "Oh, I haven't thought about God for the last hour."

In the beginning you might not even think of God from the time you went to bed at night until you awakened in the morning. Later on you will be shocked at yourself if that happens, because you will know that you cannot close your eyes to God for eight, nine, or ten hours. You must awaken sometime during the night until the day comes when you can be communing with God in your sleep. Years and years of this practice are necessary before you can go to sleep meditating, and keep on meditating right through the night, or through as much of the night as is necessary.

Practicing the Presence Leads to Communion

From practicing the presence of God, we go to a second stage, and that is communing with God. The day comes when the practice of God is not done through conscious thinking; you do not have to remind yourself of these truths any more. They automatically keep coming into your thought, and they come spontaneously, not through a conscious act.

Right now I am looking through the window into a garden where there is a huge mass of beautiful flowers and foliage. At my first glimpse of it as I sat here this afternoon, a quotation sprang into my head, "The fool hath said in his heart, There is no God."[9] I did not have to think that. That was a passage from the Bible that came to me spontaneously. It was practicing the presence of God, my acknowledgment of God's presence and power appearing as such beauty.

When I sit at my meals, I do not have to say grace consciously or say, "Thank You, Father." As a matter of fact, in our family as we sit at the table, and because occasionally others are there, we have the practice of just a side comment which no one can recognize as an acknowledgment of Grace. It means that each one of us at the table is automatically saying grace, that is, recognizing God as the substance of what is appearing on our table.

It is at this stage, when the conscious acknowledgment of God has resolved itself into an almost involuntary act that communion with God becomes possible. The presence of God has become so real that when you sit down and close your eyes, instantly you feel Something within you, and it is almost as if you were holding a conversation with God.

At times situations of a somewhat unpleasant nature have arisen in my experience in connection with the work when I have found it possible to turn within and say, "Father, look, if You don't like me in this job, kick me out." And there was not anything of the smart aleck about that, because I was not doing it in public for observation. It was an inner communion, but because of an established relationship with God I could speak that way to the Father.

There have been other times when there was such a warmth and gentleness that I could sit without words, without thoughts, basking in it, just enjoying the reassurance of the inner Presence. You might call it a state of grace, because it was a total detachment from concern about any person, situation, or condition, as if living really in a bubble completely cut off from the world, and yet able to look out through the bubble at the world without any reaction.

Be Patient with Yourself When That Sense of Separation Comes

In the first years of communion, the Presence is not always there and one has to learn to meditate and to be patient. If It does not come in five or ten minutes and you have something else to do, go and do it, and do not be concerned or disappointed. Return, however, at the first opportunity and try it again. If you have a half hour at another time and the awareness does not come immediately, wait and be patient, not necessarily with eyes closed for the whole half hour, but meditate for three or four minutes. Then open the eyes and sit quietly for a while, meditate again, open the eyes and even pick up a book and read something that will keep thought on the spiritual level. Let a half hour or an hour pass, reading, meditating, sometimes even taking a nap, and begin all over again. If it still does not come, learn not to be disappointed. Try it again at night; try it the next day. If three days go by, or five days, learn to be patient; try not to have the feeling, "Oh, God, have You deserted me?" No, no, no. Maintain an absolute confidence that God is there.

Perhaps there is no particular occasion for any experience of communion at the moment. Then in due time it returns again.

The periods of conscious communion may, of course, be two, three, or ten times in a day, and then there may be ten days without a sign, or thirty. As a rule, however, there is at least some kind of response within that gives you the assurance that you are not cut off from God. As the years go on, communion with God becomes more and more a frequent experience until the day comes when it is a constant experience, and a whole year—even three years—goes by without ever knowing a single lapse or break in that communion.

Then for no reason at all, a break comes. It seems for a while as if you are cut off. Those are unpleasant moments, unpleasant days, but you have to learn to keep your mouth closed and not complain to anybody. If your disposition gets nasty, stay indoors and away from people so that you do not exhibit it, because someone will say that you are not a very good example of a God-conscious person. You cannot tell him that at that particular moment you are not conscious of God: you have almost found His son Beelzebub!

I do not know that the day ever comes in our human experience when it can be said that forever and forever and forever there is no sense of separation from God, for I truthfully have not attained any such stage. I have had long periods without knowing a single minute of a sense of separation, but then I have had plenty of times when there was that sense of separation. There was no real separation. God never deserted me, but there have been periods when I could not feel that Presence, and I was miserable.

Conscious Union

In place of the continuous awareness of the Presence something greater comes, for now the third stage, conscious union with God, begins. That, of course, is not a continuing experience with anyone, not even with Jesus Christ. Did not Jesus have to go away for forty days to a mountain? Did he not have to leave the disciples for certain periods to be alone? The sense of conscious union with God comes and goes, and in the moments of its coming, there is not even a you. You have so completely been dissolved that there is really only a realization that God is there and not you.

Those periods come to me often. That is the joy of my life, for it is then that all the revelations that have come to me have taken place. They have come to me while I was teaching; they have come in the form of unfoldments that I did not know before. I learned them at the same time that they came through my mouth.

I could tell you story after story about how the messages that make up the various books and pamphlets of the Infinite Way have come through—not from things that I knew, but from things that came to me when I was "absent from the body, and. . . present with the Lord."[10] Those are the moments, not of communion, because in communion there are two of us, but of union when there is only One, and Joel is not there, but *I* am there. To attain that consciousness and eventually to retain it is the ultimate goal of our work, just as we retain, at least for most of the time, the periods of communion.

When the I Is Lifted Up

I have learned that it is easier for me to be in the Spirit and remain in It if I am with those who are, or who are attempting to be, in and of the Spirit. Where two or more are gathered together, not wanting anything in this world but communion with God, it is much easier than when I am alone.

Another thing I have discovered is that if I can be in the Presence of someone who has gone beyond me in realization, that person can lift me even higher than I can go by myself. So, too, I have learned that I can take a student a hundred years forward in one year, just by his being with me and meditating with me. It lifts the student to a degree that he cannot lift himself. Those of you who have meditated with me in groups or individually know how easy and simple it is to relax into meditation, and yet a day or two later, when you try it by yourself, how difficult it is.

The answer is: "And I, if I be lifted up from the earth, will draw all men unto me."[11] If Jesus Christ were on earth today, I can assure you that I would move wherever he was living, and I would not care whether he spoke to me or had time for me. As long as I could be within range of his consciousness, I know that he could lift me higher than my own. With our students I have had the experience that those who are with me more of the time than the others are the ones who rise higher and remain higher.

That really is not a leaning on others, nor is it borrowing their light. It is the same in the spiritual world as with flowers and the sunshine. When the sun produces a heat of only 50 degrees, results from your garden are not as satisfactory as when the temperature goes to 60, 70, 72, or 80 degrees. The degree of light and warmth that is radiated into the garden gives the flowers better coloring and form.

Your consciousness and mine are already infinite, but you are not showing that forth any more than I am. We are showing forth only a degree of that infinity. Therefore, whenever I can be in the company of men and women who are dedicating their lives to God, if they are in some manner living the Christ-way, I seek them out, because I enjoy their companionship and I benefit by it, and many of them have told me how they benefit by being with me for the same reason.

Living and moving in a spiritual atmosphere continuously, more of the Spirit comes through. It is not I. It could not be. Jesus made that clear: "I can of mine own self do nothing."[12] But in the degree that I and the Father are one, that light pours forth.

How else do you think it was possible for Jesus to take

twelve ignorant fishermen, one a tax collector, and in a short time send them out as healers and teachers of his message? Do you think that he could humanly teach them enough to do that? No. By his Spirit he lifted his disciples and they acknowledged it: "'In the name of the Lord Jesus,'[13] in the consciousness of the Christ, this is being done. Through the Spirit these works are being done." But later they had to stand on their own consciousness because he said to them, "If I go not away, the Comforter will not come unto you."[14] There does come a time when you have to recognize God as your individual being.

Even when you do, you will never neglect an opportunity to commune with men and women on the spiritual path. You will not care whether they are rabbis, priests, ministers, swamis, evangelical healers, what they are or who they are, as long as they are dedicated souls, not just people walking around pretending to be something they have not attained.

I have met people all over the world who are dedicated, who are called. Some of them continue to work in orthodox churches, temples, or synagogues. Others work independently. But they all have that mind which was in Christ Jesus. Rest assured of this, we need fellowship with those of that mind. We need each other. Where two or more are gathered together in this consciousness, there the Christ is more strongly manifest than when one is alone.

Conscious Oneness Brings Oneness with All Spiritual Being

Sometimes in the beginning we have to take a stand intellectually that we have not attained, that is, we have to bring to our conscious remembrance certain statements that we expect to prove but which we have not yet proved, and by keeping these in consciousness, we lift ourselves to the place of realization. One such statement is, "My oneness with God constitutes my oneness with all spiritual being and idea,"[15] the theme of the book *Conscious Union With God*. Think what that statement means! If I am consciously one with God, I am consciously at one with every individual, every place, and everything necessary to my unfoldment, or everyone whom I can help in his unfoldment. Is it not true that without any human means whatsoever you were drawn to this letter, because you, having prayed for truth, have been attuned to the consciousness where you can receive it? I, by my conscious oneness with God have been drawn to you, where each of us is serving the other in one way or another.

If it were a flower that you needed, your conscious union with God would bring that flower to you. If it were a dollar or a pound, that conscious union with God would bring the dollar or the pound, or as many as were necessary. If it were a home, if it were transportation, if it were anything necessary to your experience, your conscious union with God would be your conscious oneness with all forms of good.

Once you understand this point, you will see why it is necessary day after day to remind yourself, "My conscious oneness with God is my only demonstration. When I have made that, all things are added unto me. Nothing do I have to seek: place, position, power, name, fame, glory, money, home, companionship—none of these. They are all added unto me."

The Light of the Teacher
Lights the Way

The teacher can reveal to the student the revelations that have come to the teacher. Through his uplifted consciousness, the student can be lifted up in some measure. But from there on the responsibility is with the student. There is nobody to lean on. Through his own conscious effort, through his devotion, through his study, through his practice, through his meditation, each one individually must demonstrate consciously his oneness with God. That is why the Infinite Way path is such a difficult one.

The teacher can reveal to you the footsteps leading to the goal and, by working with you individually and collectively, can lift you up a step toward the goal, but from then on you have to take over and complete the demonstration for yourself. It is not given to anyone on the face of the globe, and it never has been, to walk on the water for another. Peter had to learn to walk on the water alone. The disciples had to learn to go out without money and without scrip and demonstrate their supply. They had to go out into the world and demonstrate their protection, and the Master was not around after the crucifixion to do it for them. They had three years of continuous, close instruction, and then they were thrown on their own.

Except for the few, no one has three years of constant, close contact with the teacher, but then he has more than three years with other students on the path, which helps to make up for it. It enables the students to take the periods in between the personal contact to evolve to a greater extent than they are at any given moment of contact with the teacher and prepare themselves for the next step.

As a Preparation
Forsake Human Demonstration

To assimilate truth there must be a readiness and a preparation for it. The Master illustrated that with the three states of consciousness: the stony soil, the barren soil, the fertile soil. This message could never be given to those who have not caught a glimpse of the truth that God is love, and not only that God is love, but that God is omnipresence. But the responsibility for the demonstration of this oneness is upon them.

There must be a great deal of preparation before an individual can believe that the kingdom of God is within him, because the world is seeking for it somewhere up in heaven, far, far away. So it is that students come step by step, bringing God down out of His heaven, until they have attained God within them. They then begin the journey inward to the realization and the demonstration of that Presence, and then progress to the communion and the union.

> In Thy presence is fullness of life, of joy.
> In Thy presence is fullness of peace. In Thy presence
> is fullness of security and safety. In Thy presence is
> fullness of health, harmony, wholeness, completeness.

What is the secret then? Attain that Presence, and forget trying to attain the health, wealth, harmony, wholeness, and completeness, for thereby does the world lose its demonstration. Praying for peace on earth is the surest way never to find it. Praying for health, praying for wealth, praying for supply, praying for home, or praying for companionship is the surest way to lose it. But when you take no thought for those things in your life and pray only for the recognition, realization, and demonstration of conscious oneness with God, you awake and find that all things have been added unto you.

The most difficult part of this entire path is giving up the habit and the desire to pray for things and conditions. A person wonders what would happen if he stopped praying for supply. Far better would it be to pray for forgiveness for all the thousands of years of spiritual ignorance that have been absorbed and assimilated. Far better would it be to pray for forgiveness for acts—conscious and unconscious acts—that have violated his spiritual integrity, even though they may not have violated the laws of the land. Much more profitable is it to pray that he be forgiven in proportion as he forgives.

Once the idea is clear to you that praying for things is the materialistic sense of life, because it is praying for that peace which the world gives, you are able better to pray for that peace which the world cannot give. Then you are beginning to live spiritually, through Cause, not by the acquisition of effects.

Thou art my dwelling place
from everlasting to everlasting.
I am never without a home, and I am never
without a companion, if Thou art my dwelling place.
Thou art my rock and my salvation;
Thou art my fortress and my high tower.

Only by demonstrating your oneness with God do you have a fortress and a high tower, a place of safety, security, peace, wholeness, joy, love, and all these other things.

You have reminders of this in the writings and in the tape recordings, but you have something far greater than those reminders, far greater than the books or the tapes: you have the kingdom of God within you to which you can turn and with sufficient persistence and patience, you can break through until truth flows out of you as freely as it has flowed out of me. "God is no respecter of persons,"[16] and He has not set someone apart from you that this may flow through that person but not through you. It flows through me because of my years of heartache in which I could not live separate and apart from It, and I had to take the kingdom of God with patience, but sometimes by storming it, too.

You have the same opportunity, for God is no respecter of persons, and if Jesus Christ left us one message, it is that his God is your God, and mine. What was possible to him is possible to you and to me. Whether or not you or I ever attain the fullness of what he did does not change the truth that potentially you can make that same demonstration if you have that same devotion, and if that grace of God is with you. But whether or not you attain that fullness, I can tell you that even without it there is a great deal of joy in even this much fullness.

You have something greater than the message. You have the source of the message, which is the kingdom of God within you, and you use this message to help you break through into that kingdom.

ACROSS THE DESK

In times of problems of one kind or another, there seems to be a reluctance on the part of some students to ask for help from someone farther along on the path. If the student is not meeting the situation, it is certainly legitimate to borrow another person's light. At the moment the student may be so immersed in the problem that he may be unable to attain that inner stillness that is necessary to bring through the healing. It is wise in such circumstances to turn to another person for help, and no one should feel any sense of failure because of that.

Have no hesitancy in asking for help when needed. Never feel that you are bothering the practitioner unless you insist on rehearsing the problem each time you call. If continued help seems to be necessary, it is important to keep in close touch with the practitioner because Infinite Way practitioners do not keep lists of patients. After the work has been done and an inner release is felt by the practitioner, he drops the case, assuming that it has been taken care of.

With every call for help, the practitioner's responsibility is to recognize and lift up the Christhood of individual being and not be taken in by the appearance. Chapter 7 in *The Art of Spiritual Healing* will further clarify this subject for you.*

TAPE RECORDED EXCERPTS
Prepared by the Editor

"Sit down for as many periods a day as you can for contemplation and meditation. . . If you sit for five or six minutes and do not find your peace, don't accept that as meaning that you have not succeeded. Oh, no, because God is not a state of

---

The Art of Spiritual Healing, © Joel S. Goldsmith (Atlanta, Georgia: Acropolis Books, Inc., 1997).

emotion. You may not always have the feeling of God. As a matter of fact, I may tell you this: there are times when you are in the depths of despondency, . . . yet in that minute God is closer to you than when you are feeling an ecstatic emotion. . . We cannot always know God's presence by our feelings."

Joel S. Goldsmith, "Contemplation, Meditation, Communion, and Union," *The 1955 First Chicago Private Class*

Chapter Seven

The Practicality
of Illumination

The spiritual path is a difficult one, without any question. The Master warned about that when he said, "Strait is the gate, and narrow is the way, which leadeth unto life, and few there be that find it."[1] Indeed, very few! The spiritual path is difficult because ever since the fall of man, that is, since man entered into a material state of consciousness, his attention has been centered on worldly pleasures and profits.

From the earliest days of humanhood, dependence has been placed on might and power—bows and arrows, swords, dynamite, gunpowder, walls, barricades, fortresses—all for the protection of life and property. Over the centuries a material state of consciousness has developed, a consciousness seeking always for something out in the world to supply satisfaction, safety, security, peace, supply, and health.

When the transition is made to the spiritual path, all this has to be reversed, and that is what is called "dying daily," being reborn, surrendering, giving, or yielding one's self to God—nonattachment as it is called in Oriental teaching. All this, however, must not be misunderstood. It does not mean that we do not eat or require food; it does not imply that there is anything wrong with wealth or health. All these are implicit on the spiritual path, but without attachment or dependence on them.

Transferring Reliance from the Visible to the Invisible

On the spiritual path, all attention is transferred from the visible to the invisible, and it has been taught by the Master in this way:

> I have meat to eat that ye know not of.
>
> John 4:32

> I am the bread of life.
>
> John 6:35

> I am the resurrection, and the life.
>
> John 11:25

> Man shall not live by bread alone, but by every word that proceedeth out of the mouth of God.
>
> Matthew 4:4

> I am come that they might have life, and that they might have it more abundantly.
>
> John 10:10

It is not that we claim that protection, food, clothing, and housing are unnecessary, that we ignore these or feel ourselves to be too spiritual to think about such things. That is nonsense. But it is the Within, the inner Self, the inner Being, the inner Substance of life—not the fortresses, not the bombs, not the storehouses of food—that is come that there may be an abundance in the outer.

We understand that the source of good in our experience is

within, and as we turn our attention to that withinness, all the things are added unto us. We are led to them or they are delivered to our doorstep. The difficult part is in turning from the without to the within and there attaining contact with that Source that does supply us with everything from our longevity and immortality to our health, to the food we eat, the clothes we wear, and the housing that we require. All these become the added things after we have found that inner Grace and made our inner contact.

It is not that those of us on the spiritual path do not participate in worldly activities. We do. We do not try to live our lives in monasteries or convents, out of the world, up in mountaintops, or by the seashore. No, we remain in the world.

The Master cautioned, "Stay in the city, until you are clothed with power from on high."[2] In other words, we are to remain right where we are, doing what we are doing, until we find ourselves ordained, until we can feel that the spirit of the Lord God is upon us and we can say with Paul, "I live; yet not I, but Christ liveth in me.[3]. . . He performeth the thing that is appointed for me.[4]. . . I can do all things through Christ which strengtheneth me."[5] Until we come to that point of illumination or realization, however, we remain right where we are, doing the things that we are doing every day, fulfilling every obligation, all the while preparing ourselves for ordination.

Opening the Soul-Center

In the Infinite Way we have adopted meditation as the way to illumination. With us, meditation is not just something thrown into our life on the side; meditation is not just something we do to feel peaceful within. With us, meditation is the way; it is the means which we use to attain the inner contact. We do have a purpose in meditation; we have an object, a goal. Meditation is not that goal: meditation is the way. The goal is realization, illumination. Whether we use the word *realization* or *illumination,* what we really mean is God-contact, the actual God-experience.

In our work, an intellectual knowledge of books and principles is also not the major factor, and when we learn the specific principles that are basic to the Infinite Way message, it is not because we believe that learning them will accomplish anything of itself, but rather that by working with these principles we eventually open our Soul-center, awaken to that Giant within, and make contact with our Source.

The Old Testament God of Two Powers Must Give Way to Omnipotence

Faith does not play a part in our spiritual healing work. We do not pray to God for healings, nor do we ask God to heal anyone. Infinite Way healing work is based on certain principles that were revealed to me in connection with a long period of spiritual healing practice. A major principle is that God knows nothing about sin, disease, death, lack, or limitation, and that there never has been a God to do anything about these problems.

All the sin, the disease, the false appetites, the lack, the limitation, and all the deaths that have ever taken place in the history of the world have taken place only in the mind of man, and all because of a universal belief in two powers. Sin, disease, death, lack, and limitation are a denial of God's omnipotence. Who could believe that there is omnipotence and another power? True, there is considerable authority in the Bible for believing in two powers, but that is because the law given by Moses has been construed in religious circles as being a law of God. This it never was.

The Old Testament teachings, which also comprise the basis of Christian teaching, indicate that God is both good and evil, that God is responsible for life and for death, that God is responsible for victories and for defeats in war; and some politicians use the idea of God supporting one side over another by claiming that God is on their side. Strange how the other side has won so many elections!

Lip service to omnipotence is not the realization of omnipotence. Even the affirmation of God's omnipotence is not power. Power lies only in realization, illumination. Since we cannot accept any God except omnipotence, certainly we cannot ask God to be a power over some other nonexistent power, even though we may believe in another power. True, we may temporarily succumb to the belief that there is a power of sin, temptation, disease, lack, or fear, but if we are to pray aright, there must certainly be the recognition that we are not asking a God-power to do anything. We are acknowledging omnipotence, acknowledging that there is no other power. Because of that we are not seeking any God-power.

Omnipotence, Omniscience, and Omnipresence, Our Confidence and Assurance

How many prayers are being uttered today in which God is being told what we need, what this country needs, or what some other country needs, or some families! All of this is a denial of omniscience. It is difficult after such conditioning to sit down in prayer and almost cut out the tongue so that it does not tell or ask God something. We almost have to tear out the mind to keep it from thinking thoughts to try to gain God's power. Of course, it is difficult! It is difficult to close the eyes and realize that since God is the infinite wisdom that created and maintains the universe, there is no need of acquainting God with our needs. We must sit firm in the faith of omniscience: God, the All-knowing.

If there is omnipresence—and what else could God be, if not omnipresence—how could there be a God absent from some place? God must be omnipresence, present where we are, the very place whereon we stand. Right here must be this omnipresence which is also all-knowing omniscience, all-powerful omnipotence. What more can we ask? Therefore, our prayer must be a rehearsal within ourselves of the nature of God as omniscience, omnipotence, and omnipresence. But this is really not prayer: this is only a preparation for prayer. We must then come to the point of prayer, not what I will, but rather, "I am listening. I am receptive and responsive to Thy will; I am receptive and responsive to Thy grace." Then will come the stillness, the quietness, the listening attitude, followed by an inner peace, which is the descent of the Holy Ghost, the ordination.

> The spirit of the Lord God is upon me,
> and I am ordained. That spirit of the Lord God
> upon me is my bread, my meat, my wine, my water,
> the word of God that has been given to me by
> which I live and by which I have life eternal.

The Altitude and Attitude of Receptivity

Prayer, treatment, contemplation, and meditation lead us to an inner stillness, and into an altitude and attitude of receptivity so that we may feel the presence of the Lord God upon us:

> Now the Presence goes before me to
> "make the crooked places straight." [6]
> Now the word of God is the substance of all form,
> the substance of my daily life.

So our prayer or meditation actually becomes the experience of God.

We can prepare for meditation through the activity of the mind in what we call contemplative meditation, but the God-experience comes only after words and thoughts have come to an end and we have attained stillness, even if only for ten, twenty, or thirty seconds.

As we continue this practice as many times a day as possible, eventually an inner peace does settle upon us, and a contact with our Source is made—not through the mind, but through our awakened Soul-faculties, or spiritual discernment. Then Immanuel, or God-with-us, becomes literally true. The presence of God is with us, before us, behind us, and beside us, and we are living in and through an invisible, incorporeal, transcendental Presence about which we have heard and spoken much, but which now we experience. It becomes that in which, through which, and by which we live. It becomes the reality of our experience.

Be a Transparency for Spiritual Power

We bring omniscience, omnipotence, and omnipresence into our life as a living experience. There is then no need to take anxious thought: God is imparting all that is necessary in the way of thoughts and deeds.

This is understood better when we begin to grasp the nature of spiritual power. In most teachings, spiritual power has been thought of as something that could be used. But no one has ever used spiritual power and no one ever can use spiritual power, for if he could that would make the person superior to spiritual power. For spiritual power to function, there must be a complete absence of human power; there must be the complete recognition that "I can of my own self do nothing. . . If I bear witness of myself, my witness is not true."[7] There must be that complete acceptance, so that spiritual power can use us and can function through us. We cannot use it; we cannot manipulate it; we cannot direct it toward anyone or for anyone. We can only be the transparency through which spiritual power can flow to this world.

There is no room on the spiritual path for ego; there is no room for spiritual greatness on the part of anyone, for there is no one spiritually great. There is but one God, the Father in heaven:

"Why callest thou me good?" [8]
Why callest thou me spiritual?
Why callest thou me anything,
when all that I can be is
a transparency through which
God's grace reaches human consciousness,
and this can be only in proportion to
my acceptance of God as omniscience,
the All-knowing, so that I do not ever try
to annoy God with my thoughts, my beliefs,
my wishes, my desires, my hopes.

I accept God as omnipotence,
not as a power that overcomes sin,
disease, or lack, but as All-power,
in the presence of which there is no sin, disease,
death, or lack. I accept omnipresence.
"If I make my bed in hell,
behold Thou art there" [9];
if I make my bed in heaven,
Thou art there; if
"I walk through the valley
of the shadow of death," [10]
Thou art there, because of omnipresence.

Inbred Superstitions Are Rocks Along the Path

The religious superstition that if we have sinned God has taken Himself away from us is ignorance because no one has ever yet committed a sin so great as to separate himself from God. The most scarlet of sinners can at any moment close his eyes and recognize omnipresence, omniscience, omnipotence. Even on the cross the thief said, "Lord, remember me when thou comest into thy kingdom," [11] and found himself taken into heaven. Even at the moment of being stoned to death, the woman taken in adultery could look up and behold the Christ and be saved.

The spiritual path is difficult because there are inbred superstitions to be overcome, such as ignorance of the true nature of God and ignorance of the nature of prayer. We must be able to close our eyes to the outside world and enter the inner sanctuary of our being.

Here I am, Father,
I and Thou here together, one;
the Father within and the son without, one.
Here where I am, even in lack, sin, disease, or death,
here I and the Father are one.

The Nature of
Spiritual Demonstration

The realization of oneness operates in consciousness to remove the barriers to spiritual demonstration. But spiritual demonstration is not the demonstration of supply, companionship, or the demonstration of a home. Such ideas about demonstration are simply ignorance and superstition. There is only one demonstration to make, and that is the demonstration of the presence of God. A person seeking any other demonstration is merely delaying his spiritual progress and his physical, mental, moral, and financial harmony. Anyone who is seeking the demonstration of anything other than the realized Presence is wasting valuable time in his life.

True, there is the mental realm, and in that mental realm it is possible to demonstrate health, supply, home, anything a person wants in the human picture. There is no guarantee of its permanence, just as there is no guarantee that it will be a blessing. Somebody once accepted the belief and proved that it was just as easy to demonstrate a Cadillac as a Ford, but then he could not afford the cost of the upkeep on the Cadillac. Yes, it is just as easy to demonstrate a Cadillac as a Ford, but there are many times when we will have to ask, "What will we do with it after we have it?" This is true not only in the area of transportation. There are many things we would like to demonstrate, but if we demonstrated them, we might find afterward what a burden they would be. But in demonstrating God's grace here where we are, we leave it in the realm of God's wisdom to know what things we have need of and to supply them.

"For we know not what we should pray for as we ought: but the Spirit itself maketh intercession for us."[12] The things that have been added unto me have come without causing loss to anyone else. They very often provide as much blessing to others as to me, and I need never question whether a thing is good for me because if it has come as the grace of God it is good, it is necessary, and it is God's fulfillment within me.

Pseudo-Illumination

Illumination is the experience of God, the experience of omnipresence and of divine Grace. There are times when illumination may bring with it some kind of a vision or message, but most of what has been given to the religious world as illumination really stems from the neurotic, and many who lay claim to illumination are mentally unstable. From some of the books containing accounts of religious mystics, it is evident that most of the visions they had were in no way related to a spiritual experience. Why do I say this? Because the grace of God is not something of an abnormal nature without genuine significance, but rather the grace of God is for the fulfillment of God's man on earth.

The grace of God reveals constructive principles and modes of life. We need go no further than the Master to see that the grace of God that was upon him resulted, not in stupid visions, but in the healing of the sick, the forgiving of the sinner, the raising of the dead, the destroying of false appetites, and a code of life whereby we might live. Every part of the Master's revelation is practical; not one part of it is that of an idle dreamer. Jesus was a dreamer in the highest sense of the word, but not an idle dreamer. Every dream of the Master's was a practical dream and resulted in practical demonstrations, in life harmonious on earth as it is in heaven.

Leave the Fruitage of Meditation in the Hands of God

It is natural that meditation will bring with it messages at times. Students need to be careful that they are not looking for them, because they might try to induce them mentally and then believe that they are spiritual experiences. They should seek only for the unknown, God's grace, and since they do not know what God's grace is or what form it takes, they are safe. The same is true of meditating for the presence of God. Since it is utterly impossible for the mind to grasp God, let us not forget that if we have any thought or idea of what God is or how God will appear, we are making graven images in our mind and then expecting miracles of them, as the Hebrews expected miracles of the golden calf. A golden calf cannot perform miracles, not even the golden coins in Fort Knox, in which many people have so much faith.

When we meditate, we leave the result in the hands of God. We leave it with God to function in God's way. If by chance it brings a direct message, we can be thankful; if it brings some vision, we are thankful; if it brings a principle of life, there is gratitude. But let us not go into tomorrow's meditation looking for the same experience because it may come in an entirely different way. As a matter of fact, if my own experience is any criterion, most of the time it comes with an inner feeling of quiet and nothing more. When it is necessary, definite orders do come, definite instructions, definite messages, definite principles. In fact, all the principles taught in the Infinite Way came in meditation.

All Is Well Only When We Are Attuned to the Divine Government

Once we attain the experience, the inner contact, which is the realization of the Presence, we discover that our attitude toward life should always be receptivity, a listening attitude, morning, noon, and night, and especially upon retiring. Very often, when we are asleep and the human will is not active, when human desire and hope are in abeyance, the grace of God has a greater opportunity to enter our consciousness and perform Its work. This is why the last few moments before sleep are so important in opening consciousness to the receptivity of God. Since God governs the day, God also governs the night, but for some it may seem more natural to think that because we are awake during the day, we are more receptive to God's government. That should not be so. There should not be a split second of our experience in which we are not receptive and alert to the Spirit.

There are times in our periods of health and sufficiency when we unconsciously assume that all is well. We are physically healthy; we have enough supply; and we are as happy as can humanly be expected at home; so we accept the good picture. But really all is not well, unless we are constantly attuned to the Spirit for Its government, for Its word by which we live, for the realization of Its presence within us. Then all is well, even if at the moment we seem to be, as Elijah was, out in the wilderness without food and without a following, without patients and without students, without a congregation. But all was well, as he heard when he tuned in: "Yet I have left me seven thousand in Israel, all the knees which have not bowed unto Baal."[13] In addition to that, when he was hungry he was fed, whether it was by birds or whether it was by a poor widow or whether the cakes were baked on the coals before him. It made no difference; he was fed. All was well, in spite of appearances to the contrary.

So with us. Whether in our periods of seeming barrenness in

any department of our lives, or whether in the periods of afflu-
ence—mental, physical, moral, financial—all is not well unless
we are attuned and receiving the assurance from within: "*I* am on
the field. Fear not, *I* am with thee. *I* will be with thee unto the
end of the world. *I* am come that you might have life and that you
might have it more abundantly, so go right ahead living."

That is why, in our life of the Spirit, the moments of greatest temptation are the moments when we may be led to take
God's presence for granted, instead of continuing to be attuned
for assurance and reassurance.

Illumination always reveals that spiritual power is
omnipresent in the moment that we are absent from the body,
absent from thought—"In such an hour as ye think not the Son
of man cometh"[14]—and that God's power is the source, the substance, and the activity of our daily experience. On this basis,
the true sense of humility can develop, not thinking that we can
do nothing, but knowing that we can do all things through
Christ, that we can do nothing without the conscious recognition and realization of the Presence.

Only in the Presence of Illumined Consciousness Is Error Not Power

In much the same way, the metaphysical teaching that there
is no power in error must be carried one step further. There is
power in error; there is power in world belief, or we would not
have the kind of a world we have today. The full truth is that *in
the presence of the Christ, in the presence of illumined consciousness,*
there is no power in any form of error, evil, or discord. If the
truth that error is not power were all that is necessary, it would
just disappear, wherever it might seem to be, but it disappears
only when it touches illumined consciousness, the consciousness of that individual who has received spiritual Grace, realization, illumination.

When we have any form of error to meet, we must be sure

that after we have contemplated statements of truth that may be meaningful to us, we do not rely on them, but rather settle down into an inner peace until we feel that the spirit of the Lord God is upon us. Then we can know: "No weapon that is formed against thee shall prosper."[15] No weapon that is formed against us can prosper when we are in the presence of that divine Grace and have that inner spiritual assurance.

"A thousand shall fall at thy side, and ten thousand at thy right hand."[16] Is not the significance of that, that error is not power? It is power to the thousand at thy left and the ten thousand at thy right, but it is not power unto thee. Who is "thee"? "He that dwelleth in the secret place of the most High."[17] Unto that "he," none of these evils will come near his dwelling place, and no weapon that is formed against him will prosper. This is confirmed by the Master: "He that abideth in me, and I in him, the same bringeth forth much fruit."[18] But "if a man abide not in me, he is cast forth as a branch, and is withered."[19]

The spiritual path is an "iffy" path: *if* we abide in the secret place of the most High, *if* we live in the constant realization of this indwelling Presence, *if* we dwell in this inner experience of God, the realized Christ, or Son of God; *if* we do these things, none of the evils of this world will come near our dwelling place. But we say, "It comes nigh my relatives." "Dwelling place" does not mean a residence: it means our consciousness, where we live, not where our relatives live, but where *we* live.

The Spiritual Life Is an Individual Experience

Scripture also says, "There shall be two men in one bed; the one shall be taken, and the other shall be left."[20] Why? Every person is an individual, and he progresses spiritually individually. Individuals may unite for the purpose of study and meditation, but they cannot unite to enter heaven; they cannot unite to enter the kingdom of God. That is an individual experience of your consciousness and mine. If we dwell in the secret place, these evils will not come nigh our dwelling place, but it does not say anything about the person sitting next to us or dwelling in the same residence with us, except that a thousand of them may fall at our left, and ten thousand at our right. The spiritual life is an individual experience. The woman taken in adultery was freed, but she did not free all adulteresses; the thief on the cross was freed, but he did not free all thieves.

Life is an individual experience, as we are discovering. The secret is, "I and my Father are one," but this truth does not operate until it has been realized within our consciousness. It is true that I and the Father are one; it is true that you and the Father are one; but you and I cannot expect any fruitage from that relationship until the experience has become ours. Then the fruitage appears richly. "I and my Father are one.[21]. . . Son, thou art ever with me, and all that I have is thine."[22] In the degree of our realization of this, so is it unto us.

ACROSS THE DESK

In your early attempts at meditation, did you ever observe what it is that acts as the tempter setting the mind in motion so that the attainment of the quietness and peace of meditation is practically an impossibility? Is it not always desire in one form or another? Fear, concern, or joyous anticipation might seem more like the answer, but are not these corollaries of desire? We fear or are concerned because basically there is the desire for self-perpetuation, or that the life we seek to perpetuate be more pleasant.

As long as desire is our dominant motivation, the mind keeps going round and round as in a squirrel cage, always seeking how its desires can be satisfied. Is it an impossible dream to believe that desire can be rooted out and, if it is not impossible, how can that state of desirelessness be attained? Would it not come with the realization of God's limitless unbounded love and the conviction of Its all-presence and all-power?

For the next few weeks, in your meditation, contemplate

the meaning of John's statement, "God is love," so that you may have your own revelation of the meaning of that love. Then in the light of that, contemplate what the will of God is. The release that comes may astound you, but you will never discover how great is that release until you take these two subjects into meditation and let them unfold from within.

Tape Recorded Excerpts
Prepared by the Editor

Most persons are suffering from a latent sense of guilt about something or other, and they carry it with them throughout their entire life as a heavy burden. It is like a cloud overshadowing their entire experience. To understand the impersonal nature of evil lifts the burden of guilt from an individual.

Spiritual healing frees the individual and releases him into his spiritual heritage of divine sonship. No longer is he labeled the culprit, responsible for all his problems and having to suffer through them, not only in this lifetime, but perhaps in many future ones.

Instead of holding those who come to you in bondage to their past errors, be that healing consciousness that sets everyone who comes to you free in his Christhood to experience the glorious liberty of the sons of God.

Error Is Never Personal

"All evil, regardless of its name or nature, is impersonal. That means that it is not your wrong thinking that has caused your trouble, and it is not your envy, jealousy, or malice, not your sensuality. There isn't a single thing in you that is responsible for any of your ills, and the very moment that you seek within yourself or within your patient for the cause of the trouble, you are helping to perpetuate it, and you are making it almost impossible to be healed.

"God constitutes your identity. Your name is *I,* and you know it. You call yourself "I." The only way you can identify yourself is as I. That I is your identity, but that *I* is God. And how dare you say that It has evil qualities or propensities? . . .

"You and I may say that there are times when we feel sensual. There are times when we even feel envious. But don't start condemning yourself. That is just a universal thing that you've picked up out of the ether, and it has no relationship to you because the minute you know that I am *I . . .* you will know you have no evil qualities, no evil propensities, no evil characteristics, and that any that are within you are but the projection of that which we call 'carnal mind,' meaning the impersonal source of evil."

Joel S. Goldsmith, "Treatment and from Law to Grace,"
The 1960 Kansas City Practitioners' Class.

"The reason ulcers aren't caused by worry and cancers aren't caused by hate or jealousy or any other thing, is that error is not personal and it does not have its beginning in you. If you do not find the error before it reaches you, you'll spend the rest of your life trying to shovel all those tons of water off the desert which aren't there, all the errors and evils out of you which aren't there. Evil is not personal: it is impersonal.

"And what about this appearance, this appearance of evil, this appearance of sin, disease, lack, limitation, unemployment, nasty disposition, miserliness, or profligacy? What of it? It is impersonal, and the very moment that you declare it to be impersonal, you begin to separate it from yourself.

"When I have felt my own human errors, the human nature that would work in me, and in the past has worked to a greater extent than it dare work now, I have realized, 'Wait a minute; wait a minute: no condemnation! No self-condemnation! Remember your true identity and that this that is bothering you is of the earth, earthy. It was here before you were here, and it probably will afflict somebody not yet born, unless his parents know enough to bring him into this world as a spiritual being and never hold him in condemnation.'"

Joel S. Goldsmith, "Infinite Way Principles of Healing," *The 1960 Los Angeles Closed Class.*

Chapter Eight

Spiritual Fruitage
through Understanding

The Infinite Way is a revelation of specific principles, each of which is startling, radical, and so contrary to what has been accepted for centuries that there is little wonder that many do not understand the importance of them, and therefore the fruitage is not forthcoming.

So the question must naturally arise: Do I understand the principles of the Infinite Way, and am I practicing them? With the understanding and practice of them will come the realization that is necessary before the student on this path can experience the fulfillment inherent in the principles.

Surrendering Concepts

Whatever good is to appear in your outer experience must first be experienced within. There can be no change in the outer experience without an inner spiritual experience. There could be some healings of a mental, moral, physical, or financial nature due to the consciousness of a teacher, but that would not really be your demonstration. A teacher is only a help on the way. The real demonstration comes with your own experience, and in the beginning that experience can be difficult, sometimes even painful, because it means the surrender of many preconceived beliefs, opinions, and theories. Conditioned as you and I have been for so many centuries it is not easy to give up our cherished beliefs and to strip ourselves of them.

Therein lies the difficulty. Students can accept the new, but they cannot surrender the old; and thereby they set up a warfare within themselves, the warfare between the flesh and the Spirit, which really means a warfare between truth and ignorance. Ignorance is the barrier to the spiritual life, and what a person has accepted in mind, in thought, or in belief constitutes the barrier. So before anything else, the light of truth must have the opportunity of dispelling the darkness, the ignorance that he has held in mind.

Seeking Spiritual Fruitage

One of the most difficult places in your spiritual journey is to come to a realization that God is Spirit. In spite of the fact that this truth is familiar to you, it will become of importance only when you understand it and what follows it. God is Spirit. You have no way of knowing what Spirit means, and in that very fact lies your salvation, because if you understood it, your demonstration would be lost.

You cannot know God or the meaning of God intellectually; you cannot grasp the meaning of Spirit with your mind. Spirit is invisible, therefore you have never seen It; Spirit is incorporeal, therefore you have never touched It; Spirit is inaudible, therefore you have never heard It. Spirit is beyond comprehension, but it can be experienced. When It is experienced, you see It, hear It, and touch It, not with the five physical senses, but through your capacity of spiritual discernment or with your Soul-faculty.

To begin to bring forth the fruitage of Spirit you must remember when you sit down to meditate—and without meditation you are not going to attain it at all—that Spirit is God, and therefore the grace of God is a spiritual experience. The gift of God is spiritual, not a thing, thought, or condition. The kingdom of God is made up of spiritual activity and spiritual blessings. The grace of God can appear only in the form of spiritual good. When you pray, meditate, or commune, the only possible way of attaining fruitage is to recognize that you are going to the spiritual Source of all being for the awareness and experience of spiritual harmony.

How difficult it is to thrust out of thought such things as health, supply, companionship, home, happiness, security, safety! But all these must be put aside; they must be dropped from thought. None of them should be sought after, because God is Spirit, and God can reveal Itself only as spiritual form, spiritual activity, spiritual grace.

Go back to the teaching of the Master: "Take no thought for your life, what ye shall eat; neither for the body, what ye shall put on."[1] That certainly includes your health and longevity. Take no thought for anything that touches your human life, but "seek ye the kingdom of God,"[2] the kingdom of Spirit, the grace of Spirit, the consciousness of Spirit. Seek these things only, and then all the other things will be added.

If, however, you seek these other things, more especially if you seek them through God, you must fail. The failure of all religion is that it goes to God for material things, and of course it never attains them, and it is this failure that is bringing about a change in the religious world.

Effectual Prayer

There has been enough praying, but very little correct praying. The praying has been for victory, and victory also includes defeat. A victory for one is the defeat for someone else, and this is impossible in the kingdom of God.

In World War I, when I was in the Marines and doing what I thought was protective work, trying to realize that I was hid with Christ in God and that God was my life, one day the Voice said to me, "God must be a fool." Then I listened, and the realization came: How can God be protecting me when I am walking around with all these weapons of destruction, just looking for someone to shoot? Am I any more in God's sight than anyone else on the face of the earth? Is the son of my parents any better than the sons of the so-called enemy? Are they not merely obeying the orders of their military masters, as the boys of our parents are obeying the orders of their military masters?

A few days later came the revelation: "'Neither pray I for these alone,' but for all men."[3] Then I had the secret of protective work. To accept the truth that God is Spirit and that therefore I must be spiritual and that no weapon that is formed against me can prosper for I and the Father are one is of no avail. This is not prayer until I have turned around and included the enemy. If God is my Father, God is their Father, and if this makes me a child of God and spiritual, this makes them children of God and spiritual. And who is the "them"? Universal being! Not just Americans, British, or French, but all men in their true identity must be the offspring of God; and therefore no weapon that is formed against them shall prosper.

The revelation that because of the fatherhood of God all men are brothers carried me through the war so that I never was shot at or called upon to shoot at anyone else. Of course you can see that if this had been generally understood and realized, the war would have ended right there. No one would have shot at anyone and no one would have been shot at; there would have been no enmity, no victory, and no defeat.

Before we can bring peace on earth to the world, we must bring peace on earth to you and me. In other words, we must first prove the principle that God is Spirit and that the kingdom of God is spiritual. The grace of God and the blessings of God must take spiritual form, and then, when you and I have proved the nature of prayer and experienced the fruitage of it, proved that all the things are added unto us, our family will notice it, our friends and our neighbors will notice it, and the first thing we know, the world will notice it.

Spiritual Fruitage Comes in Spiritual Form

More rapidly than you can imagine, Infinite Way principles are finding their way into the religious and philosophical world on six continents and many islands. Why? Because of the fruitage that is already becoming evident in business, government, and health. Its work is to bring forth the spiritual experience that demonstrates beyond all doubt that there is a transcendental Presence and Power, invisible, incorporeal, spiritual, yet omnipresent, omnipotent, and omniscient.

Your meditation, first of all, is to realize that God is Spirit, to go within to bring forth spiritual realization, spiritual demonstration, the actual presence and power of God in spiritual form. You are going within for the purpose of realizing God's grace, but you will not recognize It unless you are looking for something of a spiritual nature to take place. You must not look at your body for results; you must not look at your pocketbook for results; you must not look at your family for results. Even when you come out of your meditation, you must remember that you have been seeking to realize something of a spiritual nature. Otherwise your prayer is wasted; your meditation has not been fruitful; you have not entered the way. This is a way of Spirit; this is a way of seeking the realization of the activity of Spirit where you are. This is the way in which you look only for God's grace in spiritual form, spiritual activity, spiritual abundance, spiritual love, spiritual life.

You do not think in terms of longevity: you think in terms of that life which is immortal, that life which was yours before you were born, the life you had with the Father in the beginning and that life which you will have after the experience of passing, that life which you will have unto eternity. This is what you are seeking through your meditation. You are not seeking another twenty-four hours of life or another ten years of life: you are seeking the realization of that life which is eternal and infinite.

Meditation for the Realization of God's Grace

As you enter meditation you acknowledge that the goal of the meditation is spiritual awareness, that is, the awareness of the nature of the kingdom of God, the awareness of the nature of God's grace and God's blessings and God's gifts.

Having come to that place of realization in the contemplative part of the meditation, you enter the second step or stage, and that is where you recognize that God is omniscience and, therefore, you are not in meditation to tell God anything, to ask anything of God, or to seek anything of God. You are in meditation to recognize that God is omniscience, the all-wisdom, the all-knowing. That Omniscience knows your need and the need of all Its children, a need which is always of a spiritual nature. You do not have to pray for Mrs. Jones, Mrs. Brown, or Mrs. Smith. You do not have to pray for your children. Your prayer is the recognition of God's omniscience. God could not possibly know your need without knowing the needs of all, for one is not more important in the eyes of God than another, not even the saint or the sinner. We are all equal in the presence of God; we are all one, for God is the Father, and we are the children.

The omniscience of God—Its all-knowingness, Its all-wisdom—assures you that God knows you are in meditation, and while you may think you have some idea of why you are meditating, ultimately it will be proved that that was not the reason at all. That was only the decoy that forced you into meditation.

The reason you are in meditation is that you may receive God's gift. That gift can come in no other way than through your consciousness when you are still, when you are taking no thought for your human life, when you are in quietness and in confidence, when you are resting in the assurance of the divine Presence. The real reason you are in meditation is that God's grace can manifest Itself, which It has not been able to do heretofore because you were not still enough to receive It.

Relax in Omnipotence

Since God is omnipotence, the all-power, you are not seeking God to be a power over anything or over anybody or unto anything or anybody. Since God is the only power, you acknowledge that there are no *powers* in heaven or on earth. Error, evil, Satan, carnal mind: "Thou couldest have no power at all against me, except it were given thee from above."[4] The only power there is, is the Father.

Just as you must adopt the principle of God as omniscience and learn in meditation not to try to tell or ask God anything, so you must adopt this principle of omnipotence and relax. There are no other powers. There is no power in sin, no power in false appetite, no power in disease, no power in the universal beliefs of this world. All power is in God, and if you would be spiritually fed, you must acknowledge and accept this, and stop fighting evil powers:

> "Resist not evil," [5] for *I* in the midst of thee am the
> all-power, the only power. "No weapon that is
> formed against thee shall prosper,"[6] because weapons
> have no more power than human belief gives them.

When you acknowledge omnipotence, you are taking from human belief its power.

For many days and many weeks be prepared to meditate on the subject of omniscience before you really gain an inner response that assures you, "That is it! Never again will I reach up to God for anything, knowing that God has reached me beforehand." So, too, it may be many days, weeks, and perhaps months before you attain the actual consciousness that God is omnipotence, so that you can look out on all the so-called powers of this world in the same way that you would look out on the illusion in the desert and say, "Oh, I recognize you: illusion, appearance, not reality, not presence, not power."

No Escape from Omnipresence

You, along with everyone else, have been misled into believing that under certain conditions God is not present with you. If, for some reason of ignorance, you have sinned, do not believe that God has abandoned you. Do not accept it. God is omnipresence, and therefore, there is no escaping God, not even in sin. Or perhaps you have believed that there is some incurable disease and that this proves the absence of God. Do not believe it. The very belief in the absence of God perpetuates the belief in the presence and power of disease. Acknowledge Omnipresence, even if you are making your bed in hell:

> Here where I am, God is. In spite of my sin, in spite
> of my disease, in spite of my lack or limitation, in
> spite of my unhappiness, God is omnipresent.

In the moment that you have the actual feel of this Presence, which is Omnipresence, in that very moment these illusory appearances of sin, disease, death, lack, and limitation evaporate.

The experience of sin, disease, lack, and unhappiness is due to your acceptance of a sense of separation from God, and you will discover that when you have the experience of God's presence, no longer will there be the presence of any appearance of sin, disease, or unhappiness. These will evaporate.

The truth of man's inseparability and indivisibility from God has been truth "since before Abraham was."[7] The only reason there still remains evil, so-called, on earth is the lack of recognition and realization of this truth. In proportion as these principles have been realized in consciousness, men throughout all ages have found their spiritual freedom.

Sometimes the question is asked, "Why are so many people who have realized God still battling with the evils of this world?" The answer is that the tacit acceptance of the universal belief in two powers still persists. A person not aware of the basic principles of omniscience, omnipotence, and omnipresence may realize God, and at the same time be experiencing human error. That is what the Master referred to as "the tares and the wheat"[8] growing side by side. Many mystics throughout the ages have experienced the awareness of a Presence and Power, and yet they have gone through physical disease and material lack and limitation, all because they had not yet awakened to the truth that in the presence of God there is only the realization of spiritual Grace and in this Presence all else is nullified.

The Physical Presence of the Practitioner Is Not Necessary

The revelation of the Infinite Way, while it has been revealed on earth three times before, has never remained on earth beyond one generation after its revelation. God is impersonal. This does not take away from the nature of God as love: it increases it, because in recognizing the impersonal nature of God, there is no such thing as your God or my God, a Christian God, a Buddhist God, or a Hebrew God. There is only One: one universal God, the Selfhood, the divine Being of all.

Prayer is not a spiritual power going from one individual to another, but rather spiritual power being recognized as the quality of every individual. Even today, as spiritual healing is recognized on a wider and wider scale, it is not always understood that it is not the spiritual power of the practitioner or teacher doing something to a patient, but rather that the teacher is recognizing the spiritual power inherent in the patient.

That is why there is no need for a physical meeting of the practitioner and patient, or the teacher and student, because as far as healing is concerned, nothing takes place between the teacher and the patient: it is the teacher's recognition of the omnipresence of the divine Power.

Do you remember how the centurion appealed to the Master for a healing of his servant? Even the centurion recognized that it was not necessary for the Master to go to the servant. He knew that there was just as much God-power where the servant was as where the Master was, but it was the Master's recognition of this that brought forth the healing. So it is always the recognition on the part of the teacher or the practitioner of omnipresence, omnipotence, and omniscience that brings healing to the patient, wherever the patient is—ten, twenty, a hundred, or a thousand miles away.

If the physical meeting of patient and practitioner were necessary, there could be only a limited amount of healing done on earth, and this would make healing dependent on person instead of on principle. But now realize, "Where *I* am, he is, she is, it is"—all those who have brought themselves to your consciousness. This is your consciousness you are talking about; you are in this meditation, and it is you who are declaring:

> Here where I am, God is, because of omnipresence.
> It if were not for omnipresence,
> I and my Father could become separated, but since
> "I and my Father are one," [9] this guarantees
> omnipresence and ensures that there cannot be any
> separation between my Father and me.
>
> This is the truth about any patient or student, about
> my family, my child, or my parents. Because of
> omnipresence, there can be no separation between
> anyone or anything and the Father. Omnipresence is
> the life, the truth, and the law unto all.

You can sit right where you are and realize omnipresence for anyone in any part of the world, and your recognition of omnipresence in him brings to awareness the omnipresence that results in healing. It is not necessary that you know whether a student or patient needs healing mentally, physically, morally, or financially because you, as a human being, have nothing to do with it. Your function is the realization of omniscience, omnipotence, and omnipresence, and that Presence, realized, dispels the darkness, regardless of its name or nature.

You have no way of knowing in what manner the presence of God will manifest Itself. You know only one thing, and that is that it is not your business to know the means of God's appearing. Your business lies with the realization that God, omnipotent and omniscient, being impersonal, is omnipresent with all persons.

Impersonal Nature of Evil

Another significant principle and revelation of the Infinite Way is the impersonal nature of evil. It is natural, because of a personal sense of life, to personalize evil and to believe that evil is coming to you, to the nation, or to the world through some person, group of persons, race of persons, or religion of persons. It is difficult to unburden one's self of that personal sense of evil and be able to see that evil is absolutely impersonal.

It may manifest through a person, just as disease or poverty does, but you will never get anywhere trying to remove poverty from four billion people on earth. Today the United States is almost bankrupt trying to do it, even though many persons believe that the United States treasury is great enough to wipe poverty off the earth. Some day those very persons will wake up and find that they have impoverished themselves as well as the rest of the world, because operating from the standpoint of human do-gooders, there is not enough money, not enough food, not enough of anything to wipe the poverty-consciousness away from four billion people. It cannot be done!

Poverty can be wiped off the face of the earth only in the recognition of the impersonal nature of evil, lack, or limitation, the impersonal nature of the evils that attack the world. Let your faith be in omniscience, omnipotence, omnipresence, and in the revealed truth that no weapon that is formed against this world will prosper because all evil is the "arm of flesh."[10]

Give up the universal belief that evil is a power or a person and recognize all evil—physical, mental, moral, or financial—as the "arm of flesh," or nothingness. Stop fighting it, stop battling it, stop trying to overcome it. Rest in the peace that must come with the assurance of God's grace, and be sure that you are thinking of God's grace in terms of spiritual activity, spiritual gifts, spiritual harmony. Then you will witness that this takes form as the added practical things of life.

God Performs What He Appoints

Two passages of scripture have done wonders for me and for many people who have studied the Infinite Way message. In fact, they were largely responsible for my first trip to Hawaii, when I had no knowledge at all of why I was being called there.

"He perfometh the thing that is appointed for me."[11] At first, the only part of that passage that registered with me was the "He." There is a He; there is a Something that is about to do something or is going to complete some task given to me. Later I discovered the secret, and it lies in the word *appointed*. God does not perform for me what I would like God to do; God does not do for me the things that I hope God will do: God performs the thing that He has appointed me to do. In other words, God is not here for my benefit: I am here for God's benefit. God is not meant to do things for me: God is to do through me the things that He wills and wishes. The secret of prayer, therefore, is, "Thy will be done."[12]

I had no thought of going to Hawaii, no desire and no reason to go there, but since it had been appointed for me, that was my destiny; and as long as my will did not interfere, as long as I did not feel that I was too busy in California or somewhere else, as long as I held myself receptive, God's will was done. I was but the instrument.

"The Lord will perfect that which concerneth me."[13] What is it that concerneth me? Not my will, not my wish, not my desire! What concerns me is: What is God's will for me? What is the way in which I must go? The answer is through meditation, inner communion, and contemplation, so that I may know the will of God and hold myself receptive and responsive that God's activity can take place through me. Only in this way can a student on the spiritual path hold to true humility.

Humility is not self-abnegation in the ordinary sense of the word. Humility is not saying, "Oh, I feel so humble." True humility is the understanding that I myself am not here for any personal reason or motive, that I am here only by an act of God, since God is the creator, and I am kept here, maintained and sustained by God. I can prosper in my work in proportion as I am still inside, with a listening ear, receptive and responsive, and as I constantly remember the impersonal nature of evil, so that I never direct my thought in fear, hate, or animosity to an individual, a group of individuals, a race of individuals, or a religion of individuals. Instead my attitude is always, "Father, forgive them; for they know not what they do,"[14] and then turn within.

All these principles must be consciously known by the students and must be consciously taken into meditation day after day because there is a world hypnotism which acts upon students when they stop the process of meditation or reduce it. "Pray without ceasing.[15] . . . Abide in me"[16]; abide in the Word without ceasing. "If ye abide in me,"[17] if you continue in these principles, you will prosper.

ACROSS THE DESK

Oftentimes the question arises as to how gratitude can be expressed for healing or teaching. In discussing this subject, it should be clearly understood that the gratitude expressed is never so much for the practitioner as for the student seeking the help. A person who has arrived at the practitioner-state of consciousness and is actively engaged in the practice of spiritual healing never looks to a patient or student as the source of his supply. The practitioner must be dependent only upon his own consciousness for his supply. His giving of the help releases from within him the infinite resources of Spirit which return to him in the form of gratitude tangibly expressed.

The expression of gratitude for spiritual help or teaching is the student's opportunity. It is a part of his fulfillment. Usually it takes some specific form, although there may be times when, because of temporary financial embarrassment, it is not possible for the student to express in a concrete way the gratitude he really feels. The way in which gratitude is expressed, and the amount of it, will be in line with the degree of appreciation felt and the student's ability to express it. Only the one receiving the help can measure the gratitude he feels and then let it be released in tangible form.

Joel spoke of gratitude in *The 1963 London Work*, as follows:

"The letters that students write of their deep gratitude are wonderful to read until you remember that words spill out so easily from the pen and that when they are not backed up with deeds it is a little difficult to take them seriously. . . Anyone who receives spiritual grace, spiritual healing, spiritual supply, spiritual anything, and whose heart and soul are not opened up in love has not received the Christ: all he has received is a physical healing."

TAPE RECORDED EXCERPTS
Prepared by the Editor

Every problem we encounter always appears to be connected in some way or other with a person. There is always some sick, dying, sinning, unpleasant, mean, disagreeable, miserly, disorderly, or selfish person in our experience, or some person reaching out to us for spiritual help. To accept such a person is a violation of the spiritual principle that God is appearing *as* individual being. If God is individual being and if God is the all and the only, can there really be any such person?

This brings us to the great principle of impersonalization. Since the only individual there is, is God appearing *as,* then there is no one who can be an instrument for any of these unpleasant or disturbing qualities. They are not the person: they are impersonal.

Impersonalization

"God constitutes the being of every individual in our household. God is the quality; God is the quantity; God is the essence; God is the law unto every individual in this household. God constitutes his being; therefore, his nature is pure, his nature is godly, his nature is good. . . Whether a member of the family is afflicted with sickness, sin, false appetite, unemployment, lack, bad disposition, hate, envy, jealousy, or malice, that is the step, and it is difficult.

"You must impersonalize. You must be able to look at that individual, realizing that his nature is godly and that the sin, disease, or whatever it may be is not of that person, but is of and has its source in the carnal mind. This of which he is a victim, this which is manifesting itself in him, on him, through him, this actually is an activity or substance of the carnal mind. . . or devil.

"Now see how that violates what you have been thinking of him. Perhaps through your metaphysical background you have been looking into his consciousness to find the error so that you could remove it, or you have been blaming his religious beliefs or lack of religious beliefs or in some way or other you have been seeking to eradicate the error from him. Now you cannot do that because the error never was a part of his being. God has constituted his being from everlasting to everlasting. For this reason you must never use the name of a person in treatment, nor must you ever name the disease or the claim in treatment because you are then personalizing it; you are fastening it right to the individual you would free.

"This trait of character, this quality of character, this evil nature, this false appetite, this diseased condition, this is an activity, a substance of the carnal mind.

"Always remember that whatever belief you and I are suffering from is not your belief or mine: it is a universal belief which we have temporarily picked up, accepted, or yielded to. Never, never blame anyone, and never try to make him better than he is. You won't succeed and you will give yourself heartaches. It is no use telling a person to be more loving, more generous, or more forgiving because he cannot be anything more than he is now, until *you*. . . realize that those qualities never were of him. They are of the carnal mind, and they are not a power and never were power. They only operate because of a universal belief in two powers."

Joel S. Goldsmith, "Impersonalization Illustrated," *The 1959 Manchester Closed Class.*

"There is no such thing as personal evil. There is no such thing as evil for which you are responsible. There is no such thing as your being responsible for any of the sins, diseases, lacks, or limitations that come into your experience. It is not your wrong thinking that produced them; it is not your envy, jealousy, or malice that produced them; it is not your greed or your lust or your mad ambition that produced them. It is not any fault that is to be found in you that produced them. You have no responsibility for the evils which express themselves in your experience or through you.

"This sounds wonderful at this minute. It becomes difficult only when I tell you that neither is your wife or your husband responsible for any of the evils. The truth about it is that you are the child of God. God has manifested Its own life as your individual being. God has expressed Itself on earth individually as you. The life which is God is your individual life, and it is therefore eternal and immortal. Your mind is actually that mind which was in Christ Jesus, infinitely wise, infinitely pure. Your soul is spotless, and there is not anything that you could do that would change that because God is your soul. God is your very being, and then we will take one step further and acknowledge that your body is the temple of the living God. This is the truth about you and your life, your mind, your soul, your body, and your being. . . ."

Joel S. Goldsmith, "Three Principles and Their Practice,"
The 1959 Hawaiian Village Closed Class.

Chapter Nine

Meditation on Nonpower

The normal, natural thing for human beings to do is to think of the way in which they would like good to unfold, but this often proves to be a barrier to receiving their good. Whenever possible, a person must stop thinking in terms of some form of good and return to the idea of omnipresence.

One way in which it is possible to turn away from seeking forms of good is to close your eyes and notice that there is a black void in front of you, an emptiness. Begin to realize that right there in that black emptiness is the presence of God.

> I am looking into this immense space
> which is filled with God. The kingdom of God
> is within me, and I am opening out a way
> for the glory of that kingdom to escape.

But the space which you see with your eyes closed may not always be a black space. Sometimes it is a bright light; sometimes colors come into it. It really makes no difference, however, whether it is a white light, a rainbow of colors, or a deep black. You are looking into it with closed eyes and realizing that it is the infinity of God within you and without, filling all space.

The infinity of my good is here within.
The infinite substance, law, life, and activity of my
good are here where I am. Out of this silent Infinite
Invisible, my good appears each day, each hour of
each day, in whatever form may be necessary.

I do not know what my good should be an hour
from now. I do not know where it should take place;
I do not know what form my good should assume;
but I do know that right here where I am, right here
in this great silence in which I am, my good is.

Just as the Spirit is working silently all night to bring
daylight in the morning, just as this great Silence is
working invisibly to bring forth leaves and buds and
blossoms on the trees, so this Light, Life, or Presence
is working silently to bring forth my good.

I am contemplating God in the midst of me,
keeping my mind stayed on God,
on this all-knowing, all-loving, all-powerful,
all-present God, here where I am.
I am relaxing in the eternality and the immortality of
God. I am not thinking of conditions;
I am not thinking of amounts: I am contemplating
God; I am communing with God within me.

I am God's child, heir of God, joint-heir.
The Father whispers, "Son, I am ever with thee,
and thou art ever with Me."

And I respond, "Father, I am ever with Thee,
for we are one. Here where Thou art, I am.
All that Thou hast is mine."

Then, when you open your eyes, you are ready to take up the next work that is at hand. Whatever there is to do, you can do because you need take no anxious thought for your life now that you have recognized that this invisible omnipresence is at work.

The False Concept of God As a Great Power Is a Barrier

One barrier to realizing God's activity is trying to bring forth, pray for, or demonstrate things and conditions. Another barrier is the false concept of God as a great power which, if you could get hold of, would do all things for you. It would destroy your enemies, heal your diseases, lacks, and limitations. That concept of God has to be outgrown. God is not a great power, and God will not do anything to anything. God is omnipotence; God is the only power.

"Rise, take up thy bed, and walk."[1] What hinders you? There is no power in the condition. You need no power. Even as he stood before the dead Lazarus, the Master's attitude was: "I do not have to pray." Why? Why did he feel that he did not need to pray? Was it not because he knew that God was there before he could do any praying? Even before he could ask, before he could take thought, before he could formulate a wish, God was there.

So, if there were such a thing as evil power, God would be there before you could know about it, before you could ask Him for help. Therefore, your function is to know this truth, not that God is a great power that does something to evil powers, but that evil powers are not power. Sitting in the quiet and peace of your room, you know that the presence of God is there, and that besides God there is no other presence.

Carry that principle out into the world, and realize that it makes no difference what name or what form evil powers assume, there are no evil powers anywhere. Only the belief in two powers would make it appear that there are evil powers, but there are none.

Evil Is an Appearance, Not a Power

Anything that you have thought about as an evil power is not a power: it is an appearance. "Judge not according to the appearance, but judge righteous judgment."[2] Regardless of how evil anything or anyone seems to be, relax and give up that belief. This awareness enabled the Master to answer Pilate: "Thou couldest have no power at all against me, except it were given thee from above."[3] So look at any form of evil that you can think of at this present moment; look it right in the face and realize, "It has been my mistake calling you a power. You never had any more power than I was willing to give you. In the realized presence of God, there is no evil power; there is no destructive power; there is no sinful power because God is all-power.

Evil Is the "Arm of Flesh"

You are going to have to go through a great transition until you train yourself to stop looking to God to be a power. In fact, it may mean a struggle for days or weeks before you stop looking to God to do anything especially for you. Then see the difference when you go into prayer:

> Here I am, Father, seeking nothing.
> I do not need any God-power besides that
> which already is omni-power. I have nothing to
> destroy and no one to destroy. I can rest in Thy
> word. And what is Thy word? "With him is an arm
> of flesh; but with us is the Lord our God to help us."[4]
> Therefore, I fear not because whatever claims to be a
> power is only the "arm of flesh," temporal power,
> nothingness in the presence of God.

"Get thee behind me, Satan,"[5] you, who would make me believe there are evil powers and that I need God

to do something to them. I rest in the Word;
I rest in the joy of omnipresence. In Thy presence is
fullness of good. I seek nothing; I seek no powers.
I do not use powers; I do not use God; I do not use
truth: I rest in the Word. Evil power has only the
"arm of flesh"; it has only temporal power,
nothingness: I have the Lord God almighty.

All the so-called powers in the world are but the "arm of
flesh," nothingness. All temporal powers are nonpower.

Temporal Power Is Not Power

Pilate, "thou couldest have no power at all against
me." Bullets and bombs, thou couldest have no
power over me. Germs, thou couldest have no power
over me. This that I am facing is only temporal
power, and in my spiritual identity I do not fear
temporal power in any form. It is not power, and I
do not need God to do anything to temporal power.
It is a nothingness to begin with. It has its rise
only in the belief that there are two powers. But there
are not two powers: God is the only power.

Think how you must change your whole basis before you
can come into your spiritual demonstration. Think how you
must change your concept of God to where you are willing to
give up seeking a God-power for any purpose, where you are
willing to let God be God, where you are willing to release God
from all responsibility in an attitude of, "Go on, God; go right
on being God." Where there is a claim of sin, a claim of disease,
or a claim of lack, it is difficult not to want to get hold of God;
it is difficult to resist the temptation to grab or reach out for
some truth to use as a power. You do not need it. Temporal
power is not power. But you must know this truth:

> I need not fear what mortal man or human
> circumstances and conditions can do to me. They are
> not power. I need not reach out for God; I need not
> reach out for a truth. I need only rest, rest in the
> Word: temporal power is not power. No form of
> temporal power is power: only God is power.

The Omnipresence of Good Precludes the Need for Any Power

You have learned that God is omnipresent here where you are. In the omnipresence of good there is no other power, and therefore there is no reason to use a power. Release God; relinquish your desire for truth to do something. Just let truth be truth; let God be God.

Three times in the wilderness Jesus was presented with the temptation of two powers; three times he resisted. Do not be tempted to believe that there are two powers. Every time you go into treatment, meditation, or prayer, remind yourself:

> Help me to resist the temptation to believe that there
> are two powers, that I need one power to do
> something to another power. Let me resist the
> temptation to believe that I need to pray: harmony is
> already here. Where God is, there is peace; and God
> is here; God is there; and God is everywhere.
> There is no place where God is not; therefore,
> there is no place where harmony is not;
> there is no place where any power of evil exists.

Watch God at Work

The realization of nonpower comes about first through realizing God as the only power and then realizing that you need no power. God is. That is all. Be a beholder; watch God turn the barren branches into branches laden with leaves and fruits—but do not try to make it so. Watch night become day and day become night—but do not try to make it so; do not look for any powers to make it so. Be a beholder; watch God at work; and fear not, for there are no evil powers; there are no negative powers; there are no powers on which to use power. This is the principle of nonpower. Resist the temptation to reach out for a power; resist the temptation to reach out for a truth. Abide and relax in this truth:

> I do not need a truth; I do not need a power.
> God is all-power, and God is always God.

This is the difficult step to take. It is difficult to relax in the realization that you are not going to God for anything.

> God is. I am not seeking anything of God;
> I am not seeking any God-power.
> I am relaxing in Him;
> I am communing with God.
> I am being still and knowing that I
> in the midst of me is already God.

Be still and know that *I* is God. Take no thought for your life, for *I* is God. "In quietness and in confidence shall be your strength." [6] Quietness! Not using truth, not using God, being still! Be still!

Peace Comes When the Struggle To Grasp Some Truth Is Given Up

Do you see the peace that descends in your consciousness when you are not struggling for a truth or when you are not struggling or striving for a power? Do you see that it is the only way in which you can ever come to a state of inner peace and inner Grace? As long as you are seeking a power, as long as you are searching around in your consciousness for some truth to use as a whip or a stick, just so long will you be at strife within yourself, just so long will there be an inner conflict. You will be looking for the good to overcome the evil or you will be looking for some God-power to overcome the evil, and it will not work. You will perpetuate an inner strife. You will come to peace within yourself only when you have attained the realization of God always present, God always power, and nothing else present, nothing else power. Then you will have no need of truth or a God-power or a God-presence.

Enjoy "My Peace" by Accepting It

"My peace I give unto you: not as the world giveth, give I unto you."[7] Accept it. Do not try to use it for any purpose. Just enjoy it. "My peace I give unto you." Enjoy it now. It is a spiritual peace: it is the peace that "passeth all understanding."[8] It is the peace that shows forth the glory of God. You do not attain it by might or by power, not even by God-power. You attain it by relaxing and accepting the *My peace* which *I* give unto you.

Thank You, Father, for this divine peace,
this spiritual peace. I am not using it as a weapon;
I am just basking in it.

"My peace!" It is being spoken to you from within yourself: "My peace I give unto you." Relax! Outside in your world there are certain problems, certain lacks, but now you reverse that:

"I have meat to eat that ye know not of." [9]
Thy grace is really my sufficiency,
so I need nothing else,
not even any God-power. I have Thy grace,
Thy peace. I have meat the world knows not of.

See how the struggle goes out of thought. See how the strife goes out, the reaching out, the attempting to accomplish something.

Give Up the Mental Struggling

The Master addresses your consciousness and says, "Peace be unto this house. Do not strive; do not struggle. Your good will not come through might or power, not even through using God-power. Peace be unto this house. My peace give I unto thee." Live always in the consciousness of not striving, not struggling: *let* there be light; *let* the waters appear; *let* the earth appear; *let* your good appear. Give up the mental struggle, give up the mental striving, even for truth.

> *I* am the truth; *I* am the way. Be at peace. *I* go before
> you to make "the crooked places straight."[10] *I* go to
> prepare "mansions" for you. Be at peace because you
> will not get anywhere by might or by power.

> My grace is your sufficiency.
> You need take no thought; you need not seek for
> truth; you need not seek for powers, just rest.
> Do not resist evil; do not resist evil. Relax!

You do not need any God-power; there are no powers to fight. Harmony already is. "In my Father's house are many mansions: if it were not so, I would have told you."[11]

There is no power but God. Nothing can enter that "defileth. . . or maketh a lie,"[12] for there is no power in human or mortal thought: God is all-power. That is a whole change of base, a whole new concept of God: a God that does not have to be used, a truth that does not have to be used, a truth that *is,* a God that *is,* a truth that is omnipotence, a God that is omnipresence. Take no thought for your life. Rest in

this Word: they have only temporal power. Temporal power is
not power.

Relax in the Meat *the World Knows Not*

I have meat. I have meat the world knows not of.
Therefore, I am not struggling for any meat;
I am not struggling for happiness;
I am not struggling for safety; I am not struggling for
security because I have meat. I have the law;
I have the life; I have the substance of God.
I have meat the world knows not of.

Relax! Give up the struggle for the things of the world. Give
up the struggle even for God, and let God be God. Be at peace!
Peace be unto this house. Relax in the realization of all that the
word *I* implies:

"I will never leave thee, nor forsake thee."[13]
Fear not! *I* will be with thee to the end of the world.
There is no need to take thought for any problems or
the overcoming of any problems,
because *I* go before you to
"make the crooked places straight";
I go to prepare "mansions." You relax, you rest!
"I am the bread of life."[14] *I* am the meat, the wine,
and the water, so you need take no thought.
But remember always that *I* am the meat.
I embody that meat within Myself.

The Flexibility of Living in Is

As you accept a God of omnipotence and gradually give up
the idea of using God or seeking God for some purpose, you
will live in the consciousness of *is*. God *is;* good *is;* harmony *is;*

peace *is;* power *is;* all *is;* always *is, is, is.* That prevents your mind from running ahead and trying to do something to something or to somebody, for something or for somebody. It brings it right back where it should be, within you, because "the king-dom of God is within you,"[15] and if you would dwell in the kingdom of God, you must dwell in the kingdom of *Is.* You must live the life of *being,* not going ahead an hour, a day, a week, or a month, but living in *is.*

That does not mean that you do not arrange for all the things you have to take care of next week or next month. Those are just the details of living. But do not do that with concern, with anxiety, or with foolish plans. No matter what plans you make always hold yourself in readiness, so that if there is a need to change them, you can do it without feeling hurt or without feeling that you have lost something or missed something. Be willing for changes to take place. The more you become aware of God's grace, the more changes there will be in life, because your own will is being set aside, and God's will is being done in you.

Is God's Will Done in You?

At the present time, most of what takes place in your life is what human will wants to have take place: your will, your fam-ily's will, or somebody else's will, and you are not opening your-self sufficiently to God's will in your life. But when you come into the realization of *is,* God's will is done in you, and God's will is the only presence and the only power in you. Then God's will actually does begin to function in you. When it does, it throws out all personal will, wish, desire, hope, fear, and ambi-tion, and it brings in something entirely new to your experience.

How long has it been since you have actually seen God's will done in you? How many things can you recall that you could be sure were actually God's will in your life? You have had your thought on your will, your family's will, and your friends' will, but how much has it been on God's will? It takes discipline to come to the place where you are God-governed. To be God-governed means that every day there must be a period in your life when you consciously realize:

"Thy will be done,"[16] not my will.
Lord, let Thy will be done in me.
Make evident to me Thy will.
Clarify for me Thy will that Thy will
may be done on earth as it is in heaven,
that Thy will may be done
in my mind and in my body: Thy will!

Nothing can come into your experience except through your own consciousness. If you do not open your consciousness to God's will, you will be living your own life, and when you get through with it, you will say, "Nothing has ever happened in my life but what I or somebody else wanted to have happen, and I have not yet seen God come in and run my life." Why? Because you did not open your consciousness; you did not surrender your will. True, you may have paid lip service to letting God's will be done. You may have sometimes said, "Let Thy will be done, not mine," but then you forgot about it two minutes later. You did not abide consciously in that.

Are You Living As the Temple of God?

You are the temple of the living God, but do you live your life as if you were that temple? Most persons live their lives as if they were the temple of their own being, as if they had the right to live their own lives the way they would like. They do not open themselves consciously to realize:

God is my life; therefore, I open myself consciously
each day to God: Live Your life in me, live Your life
through me, so that I can say, with Paul, "I live; yet

not I, but Christ liveth in me."[17]
God, even this body is Thy temple.
My mind is Thy temple; my soul is Thy temple.
Reveal Thy will to me.

Be sure, Father, that I know Thy will that it may be
made manifest in me. Each morning, let me be the
temple for Thy Spirit that Thy Spirit may function in
me, that Thy life may be lived through me.

Whose Will Are You Obeying?

If you do not consciously make room for God's will to be
done in you and for God's will to be lived in you, then you are
always running around doing your will or the will of some of
your relatives or friends, trying to satisfy them and never having
time to satisfy God or never leaving room to let God function
through you.

Notice how much of your time is given to living your own
life, your friend's life, or your relative's life, and ask yourself how
many times you have ever said to God, "How about Your taking hold of this frame and living this life for me?" You will see
that you have not consciously opened yourself to let God live
God's life as you. When you let God live Its life as you, very
often you have to disappoint some of your friends and relatives.
You do not have quite as much time for them as they are accustomed to, and for a while it is difficult for them to understand
that you have a life with God, separate and apart from your life
with them.

Consciously you either run your own life or let your friends
and relatives run it. You do not consciously say, "God, reveal
Thy will in me; let Thy will be done in me on earth as it is in
heaven. Let me be the instrument for the showing forth of Thy
life, of Thy grace, and of Thy glory."

To live in this way eliminates the word *power*. There is no need to go to God for power. You do not need any powers if you are letting God live your life, if you are thinking of yourself—mind and body—as a temple of God, as an instrument through which and in which God is to live. "Thou wilt keep him in perfect peace whose mind is stayed on thee.[18]. . . Lean not unto thine own understanding. In all thy ways acknowledge him, and he shall direct thy paths."[19] There it is: opening consciousness specifically to God, to the demonstration of God—not the demonstration of things, not the demonstration of conditions or persons. Demonstrate God; open consciousness specifically:

Let Thy life be my life;
let Thy way be my way; let Thy will be my will.
Thy grace is my sufficiency in all things.

In the Silence You Find Your Good

With your eyes closed again, looking into that tremendous silence in front of you, do you realize that right there in that great silent space is your good, all of it, the substance of it, the law to it, the activity unto it? It is from this inner silence that every form of good will flow to you. Only do not outline what it shall be. Speak right into this silence:

Thy grace is my sufficiency,
whatever form it takes.
Thy peace is my peace. I have meat;
I have substance, law, and life; I have Thy grace.

Let Thy will be done in me.
Let me hear Thy still small voice.
Speak through my lips; hear with my ears.
All that Thou art, I am, for I am the offspring of
Thy being. I call no man on earth my father;
one is my Father, Thou, revealed in this great silence.

You are speaking, you are communing with God. This is God before you out here in this great, great silence, and you are communing with Him. If you have such a period every day, then the rest of the day you can turn to that silence every once in a while by closing the eyes for a second and being aware of the omnipresence of God there. That is acknowledging Its presence. You do not have to worry about Its form, just Its presence.

Once during the day you will turn to It with "Thy will be done in me," and another time, "Thy grace is my sufficiency," and another time, "Thy peace be upon me," or "Thy peace be upon those I meet. Thy peace be unto this household in which I move; Thy peace be unto this shop to which I am going, Thy peace, Thy peace," always Thy peace, and always be sure that you are allowing that peace to descend upon others. Peace is not in you just for your benefit: it is there to show forth God's glory to all mankind.

Problems Dissolve in the Consciousness of the Presence

By acknowledging this Presence, you have done away with the need for God-power. The great mystery is that when you have given up the desire or need for a power you find yourself at peace. When you are at peace, there is no need to struggle with error of any kind, because whatever appearance of error there is, the Presence within you dispels. You do not have to do it; you do not have to take thought; there is the Presence within you that does it.

The great thing is that the very moment you stop looking to God, God is functioning; the very moment you stop looking for a truth, truth is functioning, and usually the error is dispelled before you even know that there is an error around. You are not aware that error has come nigh your dwelling place because always when thought is still and peace is realized, the Spirit is operating to break up and dissolve the appearances. You do not even know that they are around.

Do you see, then, that it is all an act of consciousness on your part? You must open yourself consciously to God's grace and God's peace, and you must actually refrain from using any power over error. When you feel a problem or are aware of a problem that needs attention, close your eyes and look out into that silence and realize, "Here is my Grace; here is the substance of all that I can ever need." Then whatever is necessary to you will impart itself or will go out and perform for you whatever is given you to do.

ACROSS THE DESK

Joel had very definite ideas about how a tape group meeting should be conducted. He stressed the importance of the spiritual preparation and felt that every meeting should begin and close with meditation. Then it would be the Spirit interpreting the message and not human opinion entering into it.

It is the function of the tape group leader to introduce the tape very briefly, with little more than a sentence or two pointing up some significant principle to which the students should be alerted in the lesson for that day. But this should be very brief, not more than a few minutes, because the teaching is clearly set forth in the tape recording and really needs no explanation.

Joel was quite emphatic in pointing out the importance of no discussion before, during, or following a meeting, so that the students could carry away with them the message and it could take root in their consciousness in all its purity.

Naturally the meetings will be conducted informally with nothing rigid or stilted about them. Above all, there must be a sense of love and a normal, natural friendliness. Each tape group leader will have to discover how that atmosphere can best be achieved and pray for inner guidance in every step he takes.

Chapter Ten

Dominion

In the beginning God gave us dominion, an unlimited domination over everything between the skies and the bottom of the seas. That dominion is never dominion over anything or anybody. It is always a dominion over ourselves, and when the Bible says that God gave us dominion over everything in the earth, above the earth, and beneath the earth, it means that we have dominion over our consciousness and over everything within our consciousness. Since the entire universe exists within our consciousness, by having dominion over ourselves, we automatically have dominion over everything that pertains to our lives.

We Have Surrendered the Dominion Given Us

This dominion that was given to us in the beginning, we have completely lost, not partially but completely. As human beings, we have no dominion over the weather, the climate, food, or over germs. We should have, but we do not have, because we voluntarily surrender our dominion and freedom for a temporary moment of peace.

One of the men most responsible for the freedoms we have in the United States and one to whom we owe the most,

Thomas Jefferson, said that democracy must in the end fail, that people will lose their freedom; they will surrender it; and they have. Gradually, bit by bit, we have let somebody come along and take our freedom from us, and always the reason is the same, a little temporary peace.

We could go through one phase after another of our life and watch how we have surrendered certain privileges and certain liberties. Even in our home life, we do that, that is, the human world does. If there is one dominating member of a family, gradually all the others will surrender a little here and a little there, until the one with the most dominating personality is running the whole nest.

Dominion is something that is given to us by God, and therefore we always have it. It has never been taken away from us. The only thing that has been taken away from us is the exercise of our dominion, and that we have surrendered. The dominion we still have, and we can assert it at any moment that it seems important enough to us. Not before! But asserting one's dominion requires effort, and at this stage of experience it requires a very vigorous and continuous effort until a person is once more in possession of his dominion.

Dominion Over Our Consciousness

We do not seek dominion over each other. Let us immediately drop any idea that we are seeking dominion over something or someone else. The dominion that we are seeking is a dominion over our own universe, which means dominion over our own consciousness, over what we accept in consciousness as true or false.

As an example, let us consider weather and climate. The human race is subject to weather and climate, and many persons labor under the belief that weather and climate are responsible for colds, the flu, and many other germ diseases, all because they have given over their dominion to these. The moment an individual comes to any of the metaphysical teachings, he begins to realize that power does not exist outside in matter, but that power is in Spirit, God, or Consciousness. Then without any specific taking of thought, automatically a person begins to have less fear of age, weather, and climate. He withdraws power from weather, climate, and germs. As a result he is freer of those conditions believed to stem from weather and climate than is the rest of the world.

We do not claim to have control over the weather, but in the Infinite Way experiments have been performed in regard to tidal waves and hurricanes which have been predicted to strike a certain place at a certain time and with certain force. Five successive times these have dissolved before they struck. This is not to imply that we have dominion over tidal waves or over storms. No, we do not have dominion over weather; we do not have dominion over climate; we do not have dominion over germs: we have dominion over our consciousness, and thereby we accept our consciousness as being the power, authority, and dominion. In our consciousness we do not give power to anything external to ourselves; we acknowledge: "All power is given unto me in heaven and in earth."[1]

> I have God-given dominion, and therefore
> I do not acknowledge a power external to myself.
> I acknowledge that all power is embodied in the
> kingdom of God that is within me.

God-Given Dominion Makes of No Power Things, Persons, and Circumstances

We are not egotistical, claiming to have any power of our own or any dominion of our own, but we do claim that we have God-given dominion, and if we have God-given dominion, the storm has none. If we have God-given dominion, the germ has no dominion. God is infinite, divine consciousness, and this

Consciousness is our individual consciousness, for God has given us Himself; God has breathed into us His life; God has given us His mind, His consciousness, His awareness, His dominion. Therefore, if the kingdom of God is within us, the kingdom of dominion is within us.

I do not seek dominion over you; I seek dominion only over myself. I seek the dominion to know that nobody, no thing, no circumstance, and no condition have dominion over me, because I have God-given dominion, and since the kingdom of God is within me, this dominion flows out from me and governs my universe. I am not intruding into your universe; I am not intruding into your life. I am making no laws for you; I am making no rules for you, nor am I trying to take anything away from you. I am asserting my God-given dominion over my universe, and that sets you free to assert your God-given dominion over your universe. If each of us assumes his God-given dominion over his universe, we will all be working together. We will need to take nothing from one another, but we can share with one another everything that we have, everything in our twelve baskets full that are always left over.

Do you see why I do not have to take away anybody else's supply? I can leave everybody free to enjoy his supply, because "I and my Father are one,"[2] and all that the Father has is mine. Now I have dominion over my supply. The moment I have dominion over my supply, I have so much that I can share whatever it is I have with those who have a need of it. But then, as each one has that same dominion, he finds himself also with twelve baskets full left over, and since we do not all have a supply of the same thing, we all have something to share with one another.

Realizing God's Government

Dominion is never to be confused with domination. We have dominion over what kind of government we will have, but we do not exercise that dominion by deciding whom we want to elect and then forcing their election, if we have that power. If we should attempt to do that we may be disappointed because politicians do not always live up to their campaign promises. We will not be disappointed, however, if we assert our God-given dominion by realizing, "I do not want any man to govern. I want to realize God's government on earth as it is in heaven; I want to realize God's dominion on earth."

In our daily meditation period for the world, let us cling to the truth that we are not choosing this candidate or that, not determining which one in our opinion is going to be the best. We are realizing God's government. If we actually do hold to this, those representatives nearest to good government will be the persons elected. It may not be one entire party, but it can be the best out of two or three parties, so that eventually our fate is not in the hands of a particular party or a certain man. We must continue to realize and recognize God's government on earth, God's government of men. Then we will witness, not only a different type of person entering government service, but those who are in government will come more or less under the government of a wisdom higher than their own, even though they may not know why.

This does not mean that we have any dominion over these officials and we do not seek any. Our dominion is over our own consciousness of government, our own awareness of government, our own choice of government. Therefore, we are not merely choosing who shall govern us: we are choosing how we shall be governed. Then, no matter who is elected, we will find ourselves free, or at least more free of intolerable conditions than we have ever been before. But our dominion never extends to anybody or anything external to ourselves.

Apathy Can Bring the Loss of Dominion

One of the great mistakes made by the Hebrews was in believing that Jesus was going to be the king for whom they had been waiting. The Hebrews were no different from us: they wanted a king, and if we could have it, most of us would prefer to have someone tell us what to do, perhaps even a dictator, for the same reason. It is so easy to let the "father" in Washington decide what we should have, rather than to think through our problems and vote intelligently. So it is that gradually the government in the United States has been taken over by a little group of men, and while the people think they still have their freedom and their vote, it is surprising how little of their own way they get. The reason is that little by little they have surrendered their jurisdiction, their dominion, by just letting somebody else think for them and act for them.

We do not have to make the mistake of the Hebrews and believe that we need a king. We are not attempting to put a few men whom we like in office, nor are we, in our spiritual work, seeking to control our government or any government in the world. All we want is dominion over our own consciousness to the extent that every day we have at least one meditation period, if it is only for three minutes, in which we realize:

Thank You, Father; I am God-governed,
God-maintained, God-sustained,
and this is the spiritual truth about everyone
in our land and on our globe.

In this way we assert our God-given dominion over our invisible world, which always has the effect of operating in human experience for the universal good.

Dominion Over Supply

In the same way, why should we permit anyone to determine the amount of our supply? Why should we allow any group of men to decide how much we should earn? Why? Do they love us so much that they want to give us so much? Hardly, hardly! We have dominion over our supply, not by going out and fighting for it, not by joining a union and striking for it. This is not the way of supply in the spiritual world. Those are the human weapons that have been forged for use by human beings who have no knowledge of spiritual power. But if we understand the nature of spiritual power, we do not have to fight. "Stand ye still, and see the salvation of the Lord with you."[3]

God is the source of my supply. God is infinite;
the source is infinite; the flow is infinite.
All that the Father has is mine by inheritance.
I am heir of God to all of the heavenly riches.

In such a meditation we are not trying to take anything away from any person. We are asserting our God-given dominion over supply; we are asserting our spiritual right to the infinite supply of God. Then we watch as it unfolds on the human plane. Eventually, if we maintain our spiritual dominion, our supply and our opportunities must increase. Something must increase because it is God's will that we have abundance and that we have twelve baskets full left over to share with others.

Probably we lose part of our dominion by thinking in terms of yesterday's manna—yesterday's avenue of supply or yesterday's limitation—instead of taking each day as it comes, realizing that this is the day the Lord has made, the day in which we are one with the Father and all that the Father has is ours, and then living each day in that consciousness, watching the flow begin to move in our direction.

Business As an Activity of Consciousness

It is the same in the field of business, which in the human world is highly competitive. For that reason in some cases business has become dishonest in advertising its products which frequently do not live up to the full promise that is made. On the human plane competition and false advertising are the human weapons that have been forged. Not so on the spiritual plane. Where businessmen realize God's government of business, they notice how their business changes and increases, not by running around to take somebody else's business away from him, but by the normal expansion that must come to those who are spiritually guided. Many persons and companies have benefitted not by taking business from someone else, but by creating a new industry.

On the very small scale on which the Infinite Way operates, we have observed the expanding nature of the business aspect and how supply has been increased through the tape recording work, and not merely for ourselves. The tape recording manufacturers and those working in that industry benefit from it; even the post offices benefit from it. Today there are thousands of different church groups making tape recordings and mailing them all over the world, just as we began on a very small scale when tape recorders were first brought out. A whole new field has been opened up without taking away business from anybody, but rather creating new business.

Not only has a monthly letter been created that is distributed among English speaking people throughout the world, but it is also published in German, French, and Dutch editions, all creating new business. Now other metaphysical movements are issuing monthly letters. So it is that business increases by the creation of new ideas. Our monthly letter was a new idea; the tape recording was a new one; and could we think that our Father does not have a million other new ideas? Of course! God is infinite, and if we go back into consciousness we can bring forth as many new ideas as we need without going around and taking away from somebody else's already created activity. But all this involves the matter of dominion and how dominion is attained. How did we come to the new idea of the monthly letter or the new idea of tape recordings encircling the globe? Through meditation, and through daily meditation eventually something comes forth from within: a new activity is started or another activity comes forth.

New Ideas Always Available in Consciousness

There are more new ideas in our consciousness at this moment than have ever been brought forth in the thousands of years that men have been on earth. All of them put together could not equal what we have in undiscovered talents and ideas within us. But how are we to bring them forth? Only by a conscious effort, only as we assume dominion and sit down each day to realize:

> God constitutes my consciousness.
> Infinity is within my consciousness, and I must
> open out a way for the infinity within to escape.

I do not know what day the lightning will strike. I do not know what day new ideas in teaching, some new idea in mechanics, or some new idea in discovery, in science, or in religion will be brought forth. One thing is certain, however, it would be impossible for us to turn within to our consciousness every day for a year and not find something new flowing out from it because God constitutes our consciousness, and our consciousness is infinite.

We will not experience that infinity, however, unless we assume dominion over our time, and take three, four, or five minutes a day to go into our consciousness with a listening attitude to let it flow. Only a few minutes of that each day, and a year could not pass without some new idea unfolding, some new way opening up, some new supply manifesting in our experience. It has to be because of the infinite nature of our own consciousness.

It does no good for us to say that God is infinite. We must come to the realization that the infinity of God is embodied in us:

"Son, thou art ever with me, and all that I have is
thine." [4] I have meat the world knows not of.
I have new ideas, new sources of supply, new
experiences of dominion in me, new Grace in me.

I do not have to rely on yesterday's manna;
I do not have to rely on yesterday's way of earning a
living; I do not have to rely on yesterday's anything.
Each day the manna must fall fresh.
Every moment of every day is fresh,
and every moment of every day contains God.

But if we do not consciously turn in that direction, it is of no
avail to us. If we do not assert our dominion we will not have it.

Realize the Divine Government of Home

As human beings we could all be dissatisfied with our
homes, our mates, our children, our parents. Certainly human
faults are abundant, and eventually we could let all of these have
enough dominion over us to make our lives miserable. But if we
want dominion over our own peace, we must assert that by
going within and realizing God's government in our home,
God's love in our family: not our human love, not the love of a
wife, a husband, or of children. They may have it or they may
not have it, but we cannot be bound or limited by whether or
not they have.

We must go within and be sure that we have God's love.
When we are sure that we have God's love, every member of our
family is an instrument through which God's love flows, and we
are the instruments through which God's love flows to them.
Then they will not be bound by whether our nature is good or
bad, or our generosity big or little: they will be governed by God's
grace, not our good will. We, too, are governed by God's grace,
and not by what anyone wants to give or withhold from us.

But if we do not assert that dominion and subject ourselves to God's love and God's grace, we have nothing but human love and human grace, and sometimes that will not be sufficient. That is the history of the human race: it loves to get; it hates to give. It is only as our nature becomes spiritualized that we think less of getting and more of giving. How does a person's nature become spiritualized? By not complaining about somebody's lack of human love, but by accepting God's love, God's dominion, and God's grace. This is all an act of consciousness.

Overcoming the World Within Us

We must assume dominion over what we accept or reject in consciousness and, through an activity of consciousness, by placing ourselves under God's government, God's grace, God's love, God's infinity of supply, we free ourselves from man-made conditions in the home, in the community, in the nation, and ultimately in the world. This, however, is not human domination, but God's dominion.

Jesus said, "I have overcome the world."⁵ But he had not overcome Rome; he had not overcome the Sanhedrin; he had not overcome jealousies outside in the world; he had not overcome persecution. Then what did he mean? He meant that he had overcome *his* world, the world within him, so that he was no longer subject to anything outside himself. If Rome wanted to be Rome, let it be Rome. If the Sanhedrin wanted to be the Sanhedrin, let it be. If people wanted to persecute him, let them. He was free and independent of all of it. Only at the last when he was willing to submit did he yield himself up. Up until that moment he could walk through the crowds invisibly. He could do anything he wanted to do because he was not subject to the external world. Only when he felt that that was his mission, only then did he yield himself up and submit himself to arrest and execution.

But let us not think it was necessary. It was not necessary. That was his own idea, and because it was his inner conviction it made it right for him to do what he did, but let us always remember that he had overcome the world to such an extent that it could not persecute him; it could not catch him; it could not move in on him. It could not do a thing. It could not stop his infinity of supply; it could not stop his healing work. No, he had overcome the world by overcoming self, and that means he had allowed God to have full dominion in his consciousness.

Dominion can be achieved only by an act of consciousness. It will not be sufficient to exercise dominion just once in a day and then believe that from then on we are God-governed. The hypnotism of the world is so strong that if we do not constantly assert our God-government, the infinity of our supply, our oneness with God, soon we lose it. But we will not lose it if we persist in having a specific period of meditation each day in which we realize:

> The kingdom of God is within me.
> God has given me dominion
> over the sea, the air, the sky,
> and all that is in the earth.
> Nothing shall have any power over me
> but the God-given dominion
> that flows out from me.
> There is no power external to me
> to operate in me, on me, or through me,
> for I am one with the Father, and that oneness
> gives me God-power over universal beliefs.

Now we have exercised the God-given dominion that we have always had. If we persist in this for a year, it becomes so automatic that we will always be consciously remembering, "Dominion is not external to me. Dominion is of the kingdom of God that is within me."

Then we have dominion to the extent that the weather does not bother us and the climate does not affect us. It does not mean that we look at a bad day and call it good; it just means that the bad day can go on being a bad day without having any harmful influence upon us. It does not mean that a thousand will not fall at our left or ten thousand at our right with germs, infection, or contagion. It means that we have such God-given dominion within us that none of these things has dominion over us.

Dominion over the Body

What slaves the human race is to time and the calendar! Human beings reach the age of sixteen, and they begin to become intolerable to live with. They get to be twenty-one, and that is the age when they know it all. Then they go through all the other ages until the body begins to disintegrate. Why? The calendar says so. Where is our God-dominion over a calendar? We have it, but we have not exercised it.

If we want to go through life and maintain our body in some degree of health and harmony with all our faculties—even if we are unable to achieve the full hundred percent of spiritual perfection—we must assume dominion; we must recognize that God is the same today as when we were thirty, and if God is the same today, God's government is the same today over mind and body.

Our body is the temple of the living God, and God governs it, but not if we surrender dominion to a calendar, not if we surrender dominion to time, not if we surrender dominion to climate or weather. All this loss of freedom and well-being has come about, not because we do not have dominion, but because we have not exercised dominion.

It is not that we should have dominion over anything external to us, but we must have dominion over what we accept in our consciousness. Do we accept in our consciousness two powers or one power? Do we accept in our consciousness a power external to us or all power as being within us? We are the ones who determine this. God gave us this dominion; it can be kept only by exercising it.

No Power External to Consciousness

We are really living in a world of withinness. We are not fighting elements outside of us; we are not fighting principalities or powers; we are not fighting persons or conditions external to ourselves. The only struggle we have is to awaken ourselves to exercise our God-given dominion over our own consciousness. Then we can accept everything in the external world as an appearance and learn how to handle it. The best way of handling it is to recognize that no power exists external to our consciousness. All power is given unto us: God-given dominion over every concept, whether or not we accept it, over every universal belief, whether or not we accept it.

The human race does not have this power because it knows nothing about it. It is not being taught its God-given dominion and how to exercise it; therefore, it suffers through ignorance of its own rights; it suffers through ignorance of its own power. Everything that becomes organized has to have a boss, and that boss sooner or later tells us what to think, how to think, how much to think, even what to read. As we surrender our liberties, we surrender our freedom, and before long we begin to look outside for somebody to tell us what we should do. We begin telling our children what to do, and they end up telling us.

All the dominion we assume over others eventually comes back to have dominion over us, but when we are satisfied to exercise dominion over ourselves, then we are coming under God's grace, and we live, not by the will of men, but by the grace of God.

This involves rejecting every temptation to surrender power to infection, to contagion, to weather, to climate, to person. We have to resist the temptation to fight them. "Resist not evil"[6] is the law: turn within and realize that the evil appearance out there is not a power.

> Whether that evil appearance
> is a person or a tiny germ,
> the evil appearance is not a power.
> All power is given unto me,
> and it is not a power over anything:
> it is the power to receive God's grace;
> it is the power to receive God's love;
> it is the power to express God's grace,
> to express and give God's love.

To exercise our dominion we have to realize constantly and consciously the indwelling Christ, whose name is *I* within us. We have to recognize It, realize Its nature, realize Its function, realize why the Christ is incarnated in us, and then exercise this dominion every single day of our lives. Without exercising it, we will lose it, just as we lose our franchise of citizenship if we do not exercise it, because something or somebody will come along and take it away from us.

Nobody can ever take our dominion away from us, but we can cheat ourselves of its joy and benefit by not exercising it. It is up to us to exercise dominion, work with it, think with it, live with it for brief periods out of each twenty-four hours, instead of sitting back supinely, waiting for the world to do something to us.

When we assume our God-given dominion, people out in the world know it and soon realize that they cannot step on our toes. There is a flash in our eyes that lets them know how far they can go, and no further. Why? Because God and God's grace shine out through our eyes. It is evident that we do not want what anyone else has, that we are not plotting and scheming to take anything away from anybody: all we are doing is being mighty sure that man does not govern us, only God.

Meditation Reveals the Infinite Resources of Spirit

Is it not clear why meditation is the major activity of an Infinite Way student? The realization of our dominion cannot come to us while we are out bustling in the hurly-burly of the world. When we have had short periods of meditation for a sufficiently long time, such as a year or two, to become anchored in the truth that our wisdom comes from within our own consciousness, so that we are learning to draw it up from within ourselves, we will find that in our meditations every divine idea necessary for us to have will come forth.

Everything that is out in the world belongs to somebody, and unless we know the infinite nature of our being, we will either be struggling to take it away from him or praying to God to deliver it to us. That is not the way! The way is to discover that God constitutes individual being, that God is our life, God is our mind. It must give us divine ideas, new ideas; It must give us strength; It must go before us to "make the crooked places straight."[7]

So we go inside our mind and draw forth its treasures, first by realizing that the kingdom of God is within us and that whatever of good is to come into our life must well up from within, instead of looking out and expecting it to come from "man, whose breath is in his nostrils,"[8] even if it is our wife, our husband, our child, or our parent. Let them have what they can demonstrate: we go within.

Everyone has the fullness of the kingdom indwelling. God gave us dominion in the beginning. God gave us His mind, His life, His soul, His spirit. Even the substance of His body is our body. We, by exercising dominion, bring it forth from within us.

"My peace I give unto you: not as the world giveth."[9] "My peace" is already established within us. It is not something we are going to get tomorrow; it is not something we are going to get by reading so many pages of a book. "My peace" is established in us from before the world began.

We do not know what form that peace will assume in the

world because it is not the kind of peace the world can give, but each day let us retire within for one minute to realize, "The Christ-peace is established within me and flows forth from me." Then we discover that it is literally true: the Christ-peace, the Christ-kingdom for which so many people in the world are waiting is established right here within us. The kingdom of God is within us, and meditation is the means to open out a way for this "imprisoned splendor"[10] to escape.

Going within each day is the way, even if it is one minute, two minutes, or ten seconds at a time. But by repeating it twenty, thirty, or forty times throughout the day, we can really say at night, "I have prayed without ceasing. I have kept my mind stayed on truth." Then we find we have become God-governed through that practice. But it is all a question of us and our consciousness.

ACROSS THE DESK

Every tape group leader must recognize that the most important part of an Infinite Way tape group activity is the spiritual preparation for it. Through that preparation, a consciousness of oneness is established and the spiritual identity of every person is realized. The preparation cannot be a haphazard sort of thing, and at least one meditation period should be set aside every day for this purpose.

There must be the realization that there are not many minds or many different personalities coming together, but that there is only the one Presence, appearing as the many. Then the "two or more" will be gathered together in the realization of *I,* and each one will carry away with him the Christ-peace.

Every meeting where such a consciousness is maintained is an experience, and those attending will find healing, forgiving, renewing, and restoring. What cannot that do for the consciousness of mankind where there are groups such as these scattered throughout the world?

Chapter Eleven

Access to the Kingdom of God

The only way to overcome erroneous concepts about any subject is by knowing the truth. Error, evil of any nature, exists only when the truth is not known. But by knowing the truth about any subject you are made free in that area. If you do not know the truth of mathematics, scientific formulas, or of the principles of inventions, then, of course, misconceptions regarding them fill your thought. There is an absence of wisdom, an absence of knowledge, and the only error there is exists in this absence of knowledge.

Where can mathematical and scientific formulas, the principles behind inventions, or the principles of art or music be found? Is there any place out in space where they can be found? If you wanted or needed a new mathematical formula, a new invention, or a new form of art or music, where would you go for it? I do not mean a mere copying of somebody else's idea, but if you were really intent on composing a piece of music, where would you go? The only place would be within yourself. You would have to turn within. Why? Do you have such knowledge? No, at the moment you turn within you are ignorant. Then why turn within? Because through your mind or consciousness, through your awareness, you have access to the Infinite.

If you are sitting in your home or office, in a public library or in a church, wherever you may be, you can close your eyes and tune in to the Infinite. It makes no difference what you may be seeking. As long as it is in the realm of the mental or spiritual, you can turn within, and what you bring forth from within can be externalized in mental or material form, as the need may be. It can externalize in the form of a machine, a formula, an invention, a discovery, or a composition, but before it can appear externally, you have to go within for the principle, for the awareness, for the understanding.

Spiritual Principles Unfold from Within

In our work we are thinking in terms of the spiritual; and therefore, we are likely to think in terms of men like Lao-tse, Buddha, Moses, Elijah, Isaiah, Jesus, or Shankara. Where did these men get their great spiritual power and their great spiritual wisdom, a wisdom that, handed down in the form of manuscripts, has come down through thousands of years of time?

Those of you who have seen the pyramids and temples of Egypt know that some of the great architectural wisdom that today we consider to be important existed 4000 years B.C. How, then, did these men of ancient times attain that wisdom? Where from? Those were the days before books, before libraries, before what we know as scientific research. The answer is that men had access to the Infinite through their own consciousness. They turned within, tuned in, and brought forth the spiritual wisdom by which we live today.

Lao-tse brought through the principle of nonresistance. He gave the illustration of a stream of running water meeting with obstructions. It overcomes every obstruction, sometimes by going over, sometimes by plowing under, sometimes by going around, but always without struggle the stream of running water finds its way past all obstacles.

Buddha gave to the world probably one of the greatest principles that has so far been revealed, the principle which has to do with the illusory nature of appearances, the illusory nature of what we call material and mental forces and powers. Through the realization of this one principle brought forth by Gautama from the Buddha-mind, or divine Consciousness, man could live absolutely free of the fear of sin, disease, death, or poverty. This was revealed to Buddha by the simple act of meditating. He had already discovered that there was no use in starving one's self, fasting, or dieting; he had discovered there was no use of asceticism or sacrifice in any form. Therefore, he could sit and meditate quietly and peacefully.

In quietness and in confidence Buddha turned within and realized that through his own consciousness he had access to the Infinite. Since he was seeking to discover how to rid the world of disease, sin, and poverty, he received the great wisdom: these really exist only in the mind of men as illusory concepts. As such, they have no power; they have no presence; they cannot maintain themselves or perpetuate themselves because they have no law. There is no law of error, no law of evil. Therefore, relax, be at peace, and discover that harmony is ever with you once you have learned this truth. Knowing the illusory nature of appearances makes you free of sin, disease, death, lack, and limitation.

Moses Discovered I Am *Within Himself*

Moses also drew on the Infinite when he turned within and had the great revelation of the name and nature of God; *I Am* is the name of God, and I am that *I Am.* The *I* of his being, "closer. . . than breathing and nearer than hands and feet,"[1] the *I* in the midst of him was mighty. Thus, in meditation on the mountaintop, in prayer and in communion with God, Moses discovered that he had access individually to Infinity. The great Unknown was revealed to him, the name of God, and with the name of God, the nature of God: a Presence within him, a Presence which was really his greater Selfhood, so that the place whereon he stood was holy ground.

Not only did he prove this on the top of the mountain where the revelation was given, but he later proved that truth in Egypt when he stood before Pharaoh. That place, too, was holy ground, and for forty years in the wilderness it was holy ground because every need was met, not only for himself, but for the Hebrew people who were traveling with him. Their clothes waxed not old, food and water were provided every day, safety and security. Through what, and how? Through the consciousness of Moses attuned to the Infinite, the Divine, so that all of God's grace could flow into and through his consciousness and become the law of safety, security, freedom, and sufficiency unto his people.

Jesus Drew Upon the Kingdom Within

Centuries later the Master Christ Jesus met not only his own needs and the needs of his disciples, but he healed, he forgave, he fed, he showed the way to multitudes. How? One lone man did this? Do you believe it? Regardless of how divine that man might have been, he did it through his access to the Infinite, knowing that as he closed his eyes to the world of appearances he could judge righteous judgment. And what is righteous judgment? It is the judgment that comes from the Infinite, and it is through consciousness that the way to the Infinite is opened.

So the Master had access to spiritual wisdom as revealed by Buddha in regard to the nonpower of disease and sin, because, regardless of appearances, he said, "Rise, take up thy bed, and walk." [2] He had access to the wisdom of Moses: "*I* am with you. Since 'before Abraham'[3] *I* am with you." That was even before Moses was. "I am with you alway, even unto the end of the world. [4] . . . I will never leave thee, nor forsake thee.[5] . . . The place whereon thou standest is holy ground."[6]

It was as if Jesus said, "I prove to you that the place whereon I stand is holy ground because the power of God is here where I am to heal you, to reform, to forgive, and to feed you." This he demonstrated and proved. It was not so that his followers might set up a worship of him. He warned them against that: "If I bear witness of myself, my witness is not true."[7] What he was saying was, these principles are not mine; this doctrine is not mine; this message is not mine; this revelation is not mine: it is the Father's that sent me. I am the revelator to this age."

You Have Access to Infinity through Your Consciousness

There always have been revelators, demonstrating that through their consciousness Infinity flows, so that they could heal, feed, forgive, or protect multitudes, not by virtue of themselves but by virtue of the truth that they, through their consciousness, had access to the kingdom of God, the Infinite, the Divine, the universal Omnipresence.

You, too, must close your eyes to appearances, turn within, and realize that your consciousness is the doorway to Infinity and that Infinity stands at the door of your consciousness ready to declare Itself.

I! *I* is My name. *I* am infinity; *I* am omnipresence;
I am omnipotence; and *I* stand at the door
of your consciousness and knock. All you have to do
is close your eyes to the appearance-world
and ignore it. Do not try to heal it, improve it,
or feed it: close your eyes to it, and *I*, Infinity, will
enter. All-wisdom, All-power, and All-presence
will enter, for *I* am here where you are.

If you go up to heaven, *I* will be standing at the door
of your consciousness and knocking; if you make
your bed in hell, any hell, *I* will be standing at the
door of your consciousness and knocking; and if you

"walk through the valley of the shadow of death," [8]
I, Infinity, Eternality, Immortality, infinite Wisdom,
infinite spiritual Power, will be standing at the door
of your consciousness seeking admittance.

Until you have demonstrated this truth in some measure, you will be occupied with proving it for yourself. Then you will be able to prove it for your family, your friends, and your relatives, not all of them, but those who are receptive and responsive and who seek you out. You are not to go up and down the world trying to save it: you are to let the world come to you and be saved. Your part is to know the truth that where you are God is, for you and God are inseparably and indivisibly one.

Allness Stands at the Door of Your Consciousness

You will notice that while *I*, God, is standing at the door of your consciousness and knocking for admittance, It is not breaking down the door to get in. That part is up to you. God will stay hidden forever unless you open the door of your consciousness and realize that your consciousness is the entrance hall, the door, the access to the Infinite. The Infinite finds entrance into your experience only through your consciousness.

It really makes no difference how sick you may be at this moment, how old you may be, how sinful, or how poor you may be. None of that has anything to do with this because nothing you have ever done or thought can act as a power to bar you from God. The only thing that can ever act to bar you from God is your ignorance of the truth that your own consciousness is the access to God, to Infinity. That could bar you. If you do not know this truth, then you are cut off from its benefits. What will benefit you will not be tithing, sacrificing, or getting on your knees, begging and pleading. Only one thing will bring these benefits to you, and that is to know the truth that *I*, the Infinity of being, the Allness of being, is standing at the door of your consciousness and knocking, ready to enter when you open your consciousness.

Opening the Door

This must make clear to you why meditation is such an important part of the message of the Infinite Way. How does a person have access to that which is knocking at the door except by closing his eyes for a brief second, shutting out the appearance-world, and turning within in a state of receptivity? To do just that is an act of meditation; to be able to wait with a listening attitude for twenty or thirty seconds is another act of meditation; to do it three, four, five, or ten times a day is a further act of meditation. Eventually to find that you can do it for two, three, or four minutes is a deeper, richer act of meditation. But everyone has to build up to that.

In this work it will never pay to try to skip a grade or to try to hasten progress, even by a day, because it cannot be done. A flower can be put in a hothouse and its growth forced so that it becomes a full-blown flower before its time, but it is not a healthy flower like the natural one that is grown outdoors and has matured in nature's way.

Just as the flower must mature and unfold naturally, so, too, is there an element of patience and perseverance on the spiritual path, because it is not knowledge alone that benefits you. It is the application of that knowledge in practice. The knowledge is only a preparation. It is the practice that is important, the ability to go within and realize, "Through my consciousness, I have access to the Infinite, the Divine, the Eternal, the Immortal—through my own consciousness."

One thing is requisite, and that is the desire to know God aright, understanding that it is possible to meet God face to face, that all the God-presence and all the God-power can flow through a person to the world by opening the door which is individual consciousness. Your consciousness is that door.

Open the door and invite Me.
Open yourself to Infinity, to Immortality, to Truth,
to Life, for *I* am life eternal. Open yourself to infinite
supply, for *I* am the bread, the meat, the wine,
and the water. Open yourself to restoring
"the years that the locust hath eaten."[9]

I am the resurrection. Though you are dead in sin,
dead in disease, dead in poverty, dead in slavery,
I am the resurrection; therefore, open the door
of your consciousness and let Me in.

If you abide in Me and let Me abide in you, if you
open your consciousness to that divine Presence that
I am and let Me abide in your consciousness, then *I*
am your bread, *I* am the meat, *I* am the way.

I is the way; closer to you than breathing.

Letting Infinity Flow

It must become clear to you that even if you cannot think
of your consciousness as being infinite, you can open yourself to
the truth that at least your consciousness is the door to Infinity
and the door through which Infinity can enter your experience.
You do not have God-power, but God-power can enter through
your consciousness and be the freedom unto you and your experience. Divine Power can enter your life, your home, your business, your art, your profession through your consciousness.
When It does, It not only feeds and cares for you, but It cares
for all those who come within range of your consciousness.

You can feed the multitudes, not by the infinity of your pos-
sessions because you may not have overflowing storehouses and
barns. But you do have access to God's storehouse, and it is
God's storehouse that has filled the thousand hills with cattle,

the sea and the air with their riches. This is greater than having access to any man's millions. Have access to God's storehouse, the whole universe, and you will draw forth treasures from the sky, from the air, from the earth, and from the waters beneath the earth, all by opening your consciousness to the Infinite. This divine Consciousness really is your consciousness, and you have access to It through meditation and contemplation.

That which is to answer you is "closer. . . than breathing" because of the word *as:* God, infinite Consciousness, manifest *as* your consciousness; infinite, divine Life expressed *as* your life. There is not God and man: God is manifest and expressed *as* man, since you and the Father are one, not two. If you use the word *and*, you have two; but with the word *as,* God and man become one. "I and my Father are one."[10] That makes all of God and man right here where you are.

You can close your eyes to the appearance-world because you are not reaching up to the sky to have God hear you or reaching back two thousand years ago to have God hear you; you are reaching within yourself. That is why a whisper is loud enough; as a matter of fact, it is too loud. Silence is better, so do not even whisper. Without any speaking, without any whispering, just by silently thinking, open consciousness. Because of the revelation of Jesus, this part is not difficult. You have his authority to back you up.

It is the next part that presents difficulties, however, and with which you probably will have to contend within yourself until you reach the consciousness of it. That part has to do with the word *is.* It is a very angelic word, but for a long while you are going to call it a devil, because you will have difficulty with it. What does it mean?

One thing it means is that God cannot do anything for you because God is already doing it, so there is nothing that God could begin today or tomorrow. It also means that you cannot bring God into the situation because God is already there where the situation appears to be. It means that you cannot attain harmony because the harmony of God *is.* The thing that occupies the mind and that you are expecting of God after your prayer or meditation already *is.* You cannot seek anything of God: you cannot seek forgiveness; you cannot seek supply; you cannot seek healing because of *is.* God *is* and God is from everlasting to everlasting. God is the same yesterday, today, and forever. God will be with you unto the end of the world. All is embodied in the word *is.*

Then why are we going to God? Just for God's impartation of Himself, for the recognition of *is,* the recognition of *as,* letting the impartation come which, when it comes, never says, "I will do something for you." It says, "*I* am with you. *I* always have been with you; *I* always will be with you." There is no such thing as the past; there is no such things as the future: all is *is.*

What about the particular sin, disease, death, lack, or limitation that confronts you? It confronts you only as an appearance or ignorance of *is.* In your realization of *is,* the picture begins to fade; the illusory appearance dies out. The law of God is functioning; the life of God is being. The law of God and the life of God are as operative in you, through you, for you, at ninety-nine as at nineteen. This realization stops the threat of death right in its tracks.

Such a realization makes it impossible for any weapon that is formed against you to prosper. None of the world's beliefs can prosper; none of the world's theories can prosper; none of the world's illusions, superstition, ignorance or fear can prosper if you abide in *is* and do not seek to have God do something to you or for you, or to or for someone else, but shut out the picture in the realization of *is.*

Omnipresence Is Your Assurance

You have been taught to believe that because you have sinned, God has not been with you. That never was true. Omnipresence is omnipresence. You may have shut yourself off from God because of superstitious beliefs, but God has never shut Himself off from you.

I have always been standing at the door
of your consciousness and knocking,
in the midst of your sin, in the midst of your disease,
in the midst of your lack; and because of
omnipresence at any time it is only necessary to look
up and be free. Because of omnipresence,
I am with you. Because of omnipresence,
I will be with you unto the end of the world.

You may make many more mistakes in the years to come, mistakes of omission and commission, but these will not remove God from you. It may remove you from God, temporarily, until you have the courage to turn within again and say, "I know that Thou art close. I know that when I am in heaven, Thou art within me. I know that when I am in hell, Thou art within me. I know that when I walk through 'the valley of the shadow of death,' Thou art within me, and by opening the door of my consciousness, I become aware of Thy presence, Thy power, the infinity of Thy nature and being." Then you are reestablished in God through an act of your individual consciousness, an act which no one can perform for you.

Even when you turn to someone for help, it is really an act of your own consciousness turning to Infinity. Every time you turn to someone for help, unless you are foolish enough to believe that some human being has special powers, you are actually saying, "I am opening my consciousness to the God that you have realized, and the day will come when my own realization will be so strong, so convincing, that others will reach to my degree of realization, but it will be through the opening of their own door."

As teachers, we are mediators to those who have not yet attuned themselves through an activity of their own consciousness, but remember that some day we shall have to say, " 'If I go not away, the Comforter will not come unto you.'[11] Let me be the instrument; let me be the mediator for you while you are attaining the ability to open the door of your consciousness and be flooded by the divine Spirit."

As you find yourself receptive and responsive to the Spirit, probably at first in small ways, you will depend more and more on your own admitting of the Divine into your consciousness, your reaching that Infinity. But do not hesitate to call for help if you do not make the grade. Eventually, the time will come when you call for less and less help and find that through opening the door of your individual consciousness you have access to the Infinite, the Divine, the Sublime. The creative Principle of the whole universe functions as and through your individual consciousness. The whole love of God, the entire love which God is, floods your consciousness by opening the door.

This is the function of meditation; this is the function of practicing the Presence. Why did the Master tell his disciples to seek the kingdom of God within themselves? Because that is where it is. Access to the entire kingdom is within you. Your own consciousness is the door. Now open it, open it by a conscious act:

> Thy servant heareth. The door of my consciousness is
> open to be flooded by Thy infinite being,
> Thy infinite spirit, Thy infinite nature. Ordain me
> with Thy spirit. Let Thy spirit be poured in upon me
> through this door to my individual consciousness.

It is the practice of the principles that ultimately makes the actual experience possible. The Master gave these principles to countless students, and many heard them, but evidently only a few practiced them. Only a few could catch the fact that within their own individual consciousness they had access to Infinity.

When the still, small voice speaks to you, It will speak using the word *I*, for that is really the name of God. Open the door of your consciousness where *I* stand, and let *I* enter, and that *I* will say, "*I* am in the midst of thee, and *I* in the midst of thee am mighty." As you hear this, it is so.

ACROSS THE DESK

At this Thanksgiving season it is appropriate to consider gratitude in connection with the tape group work. A tape group is established as an activity of individual consciousness, usually because of the gratitude the leader feels for the message. Providing a place for the meetings and the preparation of consciousness for them through meditation, study, and practice are his gift to God, to the group, and to the broader activity of the Infinite Way.

What the student who attends these meetings contributes in the form of money to express his appreciation is given with no strings attached and no ties, a free gift of gratitude. What the leader does with these gifts of gratitude is the leader's demonstration, not the student's, just as it is the student's demonstration what he does with whatever measure of spiritual consciousness unfolds as the fruitage of the tape group activity. Such money as is given to the tape group leader may be used to purchase tape recordings, but it may also be used by the tape group leader to make it possible for him to be freed of other responsibilities so that he can devote more time to spiritual activities. A gift with strings attached to it is no gift at all.

Joy to you this Thanksgiving season as your hearts overflow with gratitude to God for the spiritual gifts which He has given us so abundantly.

TAPE RECORDED EXCERPTS
Prepared by the Editor

Many terms are used in the writings to reinforce the idea of the nothingness or no-thingness of the discordant appearances we all face from time to time. Of all such terms, perhaps none is more helpful than the word *hypnotism*. To see every problem as hypnotic suggestion removes it from the realm of thing or condition and makes it easier to see that it has no real cause, substance, or person.

Hypnotism

"The nature of error is summed up in one word: *hypnotism*. . . Suppose someone comes in here and hypnotizes you, and he says that that plant over there, instead of having three branches has three snakes. You accept that because of his hypnotic suggestion. . . Because you agree that they are snakes, you go the rest of the distance, and you fear them. . . There is no possible way to get rid of those snakes, except to get unhypnotized. . .

"The minute you see God *and,* you are hypnotized. . . If you do kill the snake over there, you are going to find two more to take its place. . . There is really no claim to be handled except hypnotism. . . Hypnotism cannot do anything because it can't make snakes, can it? Hypnotism can't make anything, can it? It can only throw out a false appearance. The hypnotist can make you say, 'That's a snake,' but he can't put a snake there. . .

"There is only one error, and that's hypnotism. But if you can be made to give a treatment to a person or if you can be made to treat him for nerves, for a mental cause for a physical disease, or if you can be made to treat him for resentment or hate or jealousy or anger, or if you can be made to treat him for cancer or consumption, you're out of the practice: you're in *materia medica*. You are treating effects. . .

"Lay the axe at the root of the tree, which is hypnotism. . . The main thing to remember when confronted with the negative aspects of hypnotism, that is, forms of sin, disease, lack, and limitation, is not to be fooled by them, not to be fooled by trying to reform evil persons or sinful persons, but always quickly to remember: 'Oh, no, hypnotism appearing in still more forms—hypnotism, which in and of itself cannot be the substance, law, cause, or effect to any form of reality.' Thereby you become a spiritual healer."

Joel S. Goldsmith, "The Thunder of Silence,"
The 1952 Honolulu Class Series One.

"In Infinite Way healing work there is no cause for any erroneous condition except hypnotism. Whether it is lack and limitation, sin, false appetite, disease, death, war, man's inhumanity to man, unhappy marriages, there is no use looking into the patient's thought for the error because it isn't there. The error is in the universal belief in two powers—good and evil—which is so strong that it is hypnotic, and it makes you see pictures that are sometimes good and sometimes evil. . .

"You do not get rid of hypnotism any more than you get rid of rheumatism. You do not overcome hypnotism. You do not struggle with it. You do not look for a God-power to do something to it. You merely recognize that the substance, the fabric, of this world is hypnotism and then drop it. . .

"If a claim is presented to you of any nature and you recognize, 'No, that is neither person, place, nor thing; that's a state of hypnotism,' that is all you have to do. You are not then fooled by it. . . It has lost its power. . . When you reach a state of consciousness that doesn't get frightened at the names, 'atomic bomb,' 'cancer,' 'consumption,' 'polio,' 'mongoloid babies,' 'paralysis,' 'blindness,' 'deafness,' when you can arrive at that state where those words do not frighten you, and you say, 'Oh, that's a lie,' then you are in the healing consciousness. . . As long as these names or appearance still make you want to do something, you are hypnotized.

"There is nothing wrong with the world. What is wrong is with my concept of the world. . . Am I seeing man as a mortal, or am I recognizing Christ incarnate. Do you see the difference?

It is as simple as this, and it is as difficult as this. The simplicity is that there are only two important parts: the nature of God and His creation and the nature of error and its creation. That's all.

"If you go to the desert and see the illusion out there, the mirage, as long as you believe in it, you are fooled by it. But what happens to it the moment you recognize it as mirage? It falls away and you go right on about your business. Then it is no longer a condition, is it? It's just an illusion now. You are not bothered about an illusion, and it won't stop your progress across the desert.

"An Infinite Way practitioner does not overcome evil or destroy evil or get rid of it, but an understanding Infinite Way practitioner recognizes every appearance—everything you can see, hear, taste, touch, and smell—as the product of a universal hypnotism and drops it. This is the secret of our healing work. . . We have some practitioners who have very small practices, and they do not increase very much or very rapidly. We have some practitioners who flourish. What is the difference? . . . One knows the principle exactly, thoroughly, concretely, and works specifically with it and does not deviate back and forth. . . but stands fast until he develops the consciousness so that he is not fooled by appearances."

Joel S. Goldsmith, "The Simplicity of the Healing Truth," *The 1963 Instructions for Teaching the Infinite Way.*

Chapter Twelve

Fulfillment of Spiritual Identity through Meditation, Contemplation, and Communion

The goal of the spiritual path is the development of individual consciousness to the point of attaining that "mind. . . which was also in Christ Jesus."[1] If we accomplish that goal, your consciousness and mine will be an oasis, and all those who come within range of our consciousness will be fed, will find water and wine, bread, meat, healing, peace. Just as the Hebrews of old could go to Jesus and find peace, healing, and food, so will those who come to us be raised up.

Frustrations on the Path

Early in his work in the Infinite Way, a student may begin to feel discomfort, frustration, or discouragement. If he does not meet with some of these experiences, he has not yet gained a real understanding of the message. "Think not that I am come to send peace on earth: I came not to send peace, but a sword,"[2] but that turmoil comes, not when the student has attained but during the period of working toward that attainment.

If a student has an orthodox religious background, he has been accustomed to praying to God for those things that he believes he needs. It might be health, supply, companionship, home, better weather, or more crops. On the other hand, if he has a metaphysical background, it is possible that he has changed God into divine mind and, instead of petitioning God for those things, he now affirms divine mind. His goal, however, is the same: the getting of what he thinks he needs, the fulfilling of his human wants and desires.

But the spiritual path does not promise that. On the contrary, it admonishes us to take no thought for our life. Something that every one of us has at some time or other overlooked and forgotten is Jesus' question, "Which of you by taking thought can add one cubit unto his stature?"[3] Who can turn one white hair black? Who by taking thought can do any of these things? Yet how many are trying to *think* their way to harmony, to peace, to fulfillment?

On these two points we have either trained ourselves or been trained erroneously. First, we have gone to God for things, and secondly, we have believed that by taking thought we could attain them. In dropping both of these concepts, we go through deep waters. We go through periods of frustration when we sit down to meditate and realize: I cannot go to God for anything in this meditation. I cannot even take into my thought what I really want to go there for. All this must be left outside. I have to go into the inner sanctuary of my being, leaving the world with all its desires and its needs outside. I have to leave myself and my life outside. I can take no thought for my life; I can take no thought for my health, supply, companionship, home, or for my crops. How, then can I pray, if all these things are to be left outside?

The answer is given to us by the Master: "Seek ye first the kingdom of God."[4] This is the whole answer to the secret of prayer. Do not seek for your life; do not seek your supply; do not seek your health; do not seek your companionship; do not seek the success of your business; do not seek happiness in your home. Park all these outside, and when you go within in meditation, shut the door on the world, leaving everything and everyone outside: your mother, father, sister, brother, husband, wife, and children. All are left outside while you go within and seek the kingdom of God, seek to understand and to attain that kingdom, seek the nature and secret of the kingdom.

What Is the Kingdom
It Is Your Father's Pleasure to Give You?

What is the kingdom of God? What is it like? What are its treasures? What does the Master mean when he says, "It is your Father's good pleasure to give you the kingdom"[5]? The Father has not given us all the money we may think we need, all the health, or the home we believe is necessary. Then what is the meaning of "It is your Father's good pleasure to give you the kingdom"?

It does not say that it is God's good pleasure to give you the kingdom of "this world." The Master made that clear when he said, "My kingdom," the spiritual kingdom, "is not of this world."[6] It is not the Father's good pleasure to give you a better home, a better automobile, more business, or bigger crops. No, it is the Father's good pleasure to give you the kingdom, reality, spiritual grace.

It is your Father's good pleasure to give you peace, "My peace,"[7] spiritual peace, Christ-peace, not the peace that this world can give. This world could probably give you a better heart or more years to spend on earth; this world could give you more money, more homes, better transportation. But "My peace," the Christ-peace, and the gifts of God do not embrace any of these worldly things. Name, fame, fortune, reputation— none of these is the gift of God. The gift of God is spiritual peace; the gift of God is love; the gift of God is truth; and many other things that come under the heading of spiritual treasures.

It is not difficult to imagine what we all go through when we finally realize the futility of going to God for anything of an earthly or material nature, for those human things that we believe we need. After that realization, there comes the period of

stress and strain, even tears, until we can go into our consciousness without a human desire, without the desire for a single
thing, a thought, or a person, and be content to seek first the
kingdom of God and His rightness, His peace, His abundance,
and His grace.

The Charmed Life of the God-Aware

The entire Bible promises that when we attain the realization of the kingdom of God, other things will be added unto us.
From the time any leader, prophet, saint, or seer in the Old
Testament attained God-awareness, he lived a charmed life, a
life that really demonstrated the omnipresence of good. It is not
only evident that the Master's health seems to have been perfect,
but his consciousness was a sanctuary into which others could
come and find healing, food, supply, peace, and forgiveness.

What would it not mean to those of us carrying around
some burden of guilt for some act of omission or commission,
if we could be led into the consciousness of an individual and
there find forgiveness and the consequent peace that would
come upon us? Some of us have found such persons in the ministry of the church, the metaphysical ministry, or the mystical
ministry and, just by being in their presence, they have con-
ferred upon us a feeling of peace, a feeling of noncondemnation,
noncriticism, forgiveness, healing, and comforting.

The Christ-Peace Cannot Be Found
in Those Seeking the Peace Only the World Can Give

The goal is that you and I attain Christ-consciousness,
thereby bringing to ourselves the Christ-peace, the Christ-
health, the Christ-wholeness, the Christ-forgiveness, the Christ-
joy, and then, by virtue of our attainment, our very consciousness becomes a sanctuary into which we draw our family, our
friends, our neighbors, and all those who are receptive.

Everyone who touches our consciousness may not necessarily feel this because some come seeking loaves and fishes, and that is something we do not have to give. They do not come seeking the grace of God, the peace that passes understanding, the joy of the Lord, the abundance of God's gifts. This is what we have to share and give. Those who come seeking this find it, and then once they have found their peace, they will discover the greatest secret ever revealed to the world.

Out in the world there is in reality no sin, disease, death, lack, and limitation. There appear to be all these things, but the truth is that they exist only in the mind, and when the mind has stopped seeking things and has found a sanctuary of peace, out here there is only harmony. The whole world is as harmonious and joyous as what I see when I look out of my window on the peaceful Hawaiian scene, and yet we know that out there, there are just as many unhappy, sick, and poor people as there are in any city in the United States or in any other country on the globe. There is just as much sickness in these islands, just as much sin, and yet in this moment of awareness none of it is evident. Why? Because it really is not out there at all: it is only in the minds of those who are seeking the peace that the world can give, and they are not finding peace because the world cannot really give peace. These persons believe that so many more dollars or so much more health represents peace, or they believe that getting a new family or getting rid of the old family represents peace. When they attain what they think they want, they find they have not found peace because there is no peace to be found in the world.

Some of our misguided people are trying to find an absence-of-war kind of peace by buying the friendship of other peoples, and then learning that those to whom they are giving the most are returning the most in the way of threats of wars. No peace is going to be found in money, in getting it or giving it. Peace comes through the attainment of the awareness of the kingdom of God.

Meditation Reveals the Nature of the Kingdom of God

To most of us, the kingdom of God is only the name of some remote place, just as remote, visionary, and meaningless as Shangri-la, except that we do know that if we discover the kingdom of God, we will at the same time discover the nature of peace, harmony, wholeness, completeness, and abundance. But what is this kingdom of God? All we know is that through meditation, contemplation, and communion, as taught in the message of the Infinite Way, the nature of that kingdom of God and the treasures the Father has laid up for us will be revealed.

In meditation we discover these treasures but while we are doing that, other things try to intrude: our mother's health, our child's health, how to get along with our employer or employees, how to solve the problem of high rents and high taxes. All these come crowding in while we are trying to realize the nature of the spiritual kingdom. In moments of emergency, quickly bring to conscious remembrance:

> I and the Father are one.
> *I* is the Father within me, and this *I*,
> this Father within me, is standing at the door of my
> consciousness and knocking for admittance.
> That is the reason I am here with my eyes closed,
> my attention centered within my consciousness as
> I learn to wait for the Father to announce Himself.

The fulfillment will come when we hear the "still small voice"[8] assuring us:

> "I will never leave thee, nor forsake thee."[9]
> As *I* was with Moses, so "I am with you alway,
> even unto the end of the world.[10]. . . All that *I* have is
> thine.[11]. . . My grace is sufficient for thee."[12]
> *I* am thy bread, thy meat, thy wine, thy water.

Do not seek the external; do not take thought for
things in the external. Yes, fulfill your outward
mission; do your work to the best of your ability.
Give everything you have to doing the best job
in your present position that you can,
but do not rely on your own ability.

Look to Me within for the grace to make your work
profitable and abundant. Look to Me for the wisdom
to establish it and to gain whatever measure of
recognition is necessary. Look to Me to be the
Presence that goes before you to "make the crooked
places straight." [13] Look to Me; abide in Me and let
Me abide in you. Look to Me. Do not look to your
relatives; do not look to your friends: look to Me.
I in the midst of you am mighty. My peace *I* give
unto you. My grace is your sufficiency.

Be assured that even if you "walk through the valley
of the shadow of death," [14] *I* am with you and *I* will
lead you into My kingdom. Even if at the moment
you are going through the gates of hell, nevertheless,
look unto Me and be saved, to *I* in the midst of you.

Do not judge after appearances.
Regardless of what the outer senses may testify to,
regardless of the nature of the false appetites that may
at the moment control you, regardless of the nature
of the lacks or limitations you are experiencing,
look unto Me within you for My peace, My grace.

Seek not the favor of princes; do not place power in
those who are external to you; do not believe that
they have the power of good unto you or that they

have power of evil unto you, but abide in Me, and let
Me abide in you. Look unto Me and be saved.

Take no thought for those problems
of the world because, as you abide in Me,
I go before you to make straight the way.
I am the way: walk ye in it.
Walk ye in Me. Walk through your life
living in Me and letting Me live in you.
Be consciously aware of Me as your very own being,
the Father within, the Christ, the Son of God.
I will never leave you, but you will think *I* have
deserted you unless whole-heartedly
you are turning within, and often.

Maintaining Your Conscious Awareness of God

The mesmerism of the world will tend to set up a separation
between us and those around us unless we learn to turn within,
not only every day, but as many times every day as is possible.

Never begin your day without turning your day over
to Me. Turn within and realize that as *I* have caused
the sun to rise and daylight to come, as *I* govern the
sun, the stars, the moon, the planets, and the earth,
so *I* govern this minute of your life and every minute
of your life. Why not turn over to Me the next hour
of your life, and then a whole day?

Frequently throughout the day, we should return to the center within ourselves, if only for twenty or thirty seconds, to
remember and to realize:

I am here. Tabernacle with Me, commune with Me
for just a moment so that we may have fellowship.

The Ever-Presence of the Christ

Ultimately we must reach the goal that Paul attained, "I
live; yet not I, but Christ liveth in me.[15] ... I can do all things
through Christ which strengtheneth me."[16]

In my weakness, I find strength;
in my nothingness—in the acknowledgment
that I of my own self can do nothing,
that I of my own self am nothing, separate and apart
from the indwelling Christ—Christ is my strength,
Christ, the Son of God within me, is my wisdom.

This brings us to another difficult place in our ministry.
The world has been taught for so long that the Christ lived two
thousand years ago that it is not a simple matter to make the
complete break with such teachings and realize that the Christ
was never born and the Christ has never died. Christ is with us
unto the end of the world, and "before Abraham was,"[17] Christ
is. It takes a breaking with the past to come to the realization
that the Christ is the Spirit that was in Jesus, that even though
the Hebrews called it Immanuel, Christ is the Spirit that animated Moses. Christ is the Spirit that animated Gautama,
although the Orientals called It Buddha. But Buddha, Christ,
Immanuel—all mean the Son of God, the Savior, the spirit of
God within us since "before Abraham was," within us unto the
end of the world.

Why have we missed the way? Because worship has been
transferred from the within to the external. Worship has become
ceremonies, rites, and rituals instead of inner communion.
Worship must once again become inner communion. It does
not mean that if we find pleasure or satisfaction in the ceremonies, rites, and rituals of the church we should not have
them. Sometimes they play a part; sometimes they are a jump-
ing-off-place from which we can go to the kingdom within. But

we are never going to find the kingdom of God in rites, rituals, ceremonies, or sacrifices. We never will find the kingdom of God until we enter the sanctuary, the temple of our own being, and there find the indwelling Christ, the spirit of God. Then we can relax, and each day we can rest back in the assurance that we have meat the world knows not of.

At a Certain Level of Consciousness Material Props Are Necessary

"Put up again thy sword."[18] Governments are not yet ready for that teaching, because to take the sword from those who have no substitute for a sword is to take their Lord away from them. As long as the world needs its weapons, its medicines, its currency systems, these must remain. But to hasten the day of peace on earth and good will to men, it becomes necessary for those who are led by the spirit of God to go within and find that which makes unnecessary the sword, the outer support, the outer security.

> I have meat—I have a safety,
> a security, a source of supply—
> that the world knows not of,
> and therefore I do not have to
> resort to the weapons of force,
> deceit, false advertising,
> or any of the human weapons now used.

In metaphysical practice, there are some practitioners who have said to patients, "Oh, take off those eyeglasses," or "Remove those earphones," or "Give up those crutches," and thereby have brought difficulties upon their patients because they were given no substitute for them. It is only when a person has fully attained Christ-consciousness and this Consciousness has taken the place of the material props that he can drop them.

With the Attainment of the Christ-Mind, the Temporal World Loses Its Power Over Us

We do not say to the world, "Give up your armies; give up your weapons," even though we know how unnecessary they are in the presence of Christ. Temporal power is a terrifying power as long as it operates on its own level but, when it comes into contact with the nature of the Christ, that temporal power is proved to be nonpower. Only in the presence of the Christ can it be said, "Thou couldest have no power at all against me except it were given thee from above."[19] In proportion as we attain some measure of the Christ-mind, the temporal world loses its power and jurisdiction over us. The higher and the deeper we go, the richer our consciousness becomes in Christliness, and the less power germs, infection, contagion, bullets, or bombs have over us.

Scripture says, "Yet have I not seen the righteous forsaken, nor his seed begging bread."[20] It also says, "No weapon that is formed against thee shall prosper."[21] The world has actually believed that those promises are for mankind, or that some form of human righteousness—like being morally good, obeying the Ten Commandments, or going to church—constitutes that righteous man. There are also some who believe that the human race can lay down its weapons because there is a God protecting the world. That is why many people get into trouble. They really believe there is a God ready to help the human race, and there is none such. It is only as the Christ takes possession of a person's consciousness that he becomes immune to the lacks, the limitations, and the powers of this world, and it is only as that Christ-consciousness becomes the consciousness of the entire world that there will be a lasting peace without arms.

The Christ-Life Must Be Lived

The promises of scripture were never intended for "man, whose breath is in his nostrils."[22] The "natural man"[23] never has received the things of God and never will. The "natural man" is not under the law of God, neither indeed can be. Therefore, for the world there is no safety or security in God except in proportion as the Christ is recognized as the consciousness of man and as man begins to live the Christ-life.

It is not sufficient to know that the Christ functions through love: it is necessary that we adopt love as a way of life, and that means living the life of constant forgiveness, the life of praying for our enemies, the life of praying for those who persecute us, the life of benevolence at every level of consciousness—not only helping our fellow man financially, but more especially through prayer and communion. If we are in meditation, we are listening for the "still small voice"; we are in an inner communion; and we feel the peace and the grace of God upon us. Then all those who are within range of our consciousness partake of that, and in the degree of their receptivity they find comfort, healing, and abundance. Whatever the human need maybe, it is fulfilled.

When I am in meditation and thinking of world figures who represent the ambition, greed, and lust of material sense, I can feel, "'Father, forgive them; for they know not what they do.'²⁴ Enter their soul, enter their heart, enter their mind, lift them up." The Christ is knocking at the door of your consciousness and mine, and sometimes our realization of this truth opens the consciousness of others to receive the Christ. So the entire world in some measure is blessed with every meditation and inner communion of yours and of mine.

As the Christ enters our consciousness we will be inspired to pray for the world, to loose that Christ into the world and realize Its presence in the heart, soul, and mind of mankind, and so help to bring It into manifestation, even as every spiritual teacher brings the Christ into manifestation in the experience of those who enter his consciousness seeking the Christ. Even some who come seeking loaves and fishes find themselves open to the Christ, because inwardly they, too, are seeking something higher than loaves and fishes. But the seeking of the loaves and fishes is the first entry, and it is really through that seeking that the Christ gets a foothold in consciousness.

Practicing the Presence of God

I, that Christ, stands at the door of our consciousness and knocks, and we turn within in meditation, contemplation, and communion, realizing that the Christ is seeking entrance. So we are receptive and responsive and listen for that still, small voice, for that peace to be upon us, for God's grace to be realized within us.

This stage of our work of contemplation, meditation, and communion is practicing the presence of God. We are declaring the Presence even before we experience It; we are attempting to realize that Presence; we are listening for It. Therefore, all that we do in this period is to practice the presence of God leading up to the experience of God.

Nothing can happen to us except through an activity of our consciousness; therefore, we cannot even experience God except through an activity of receptivity, an activity of contemplation, an activity of communion. In such contemplation our consciousness is so active we have not had time to fall asleep, we have not had time to daydream, we have not had time to think of occult experiences. We have been busy with an activity of our consciousness, consciously practicing the presence of God, consciously reminding ourselves of It, and ultimately realizing the Presence, opening our consciousness that the Christ that stands at the door and knocks may enter.

All these terms, "meditating," "communing," "contemplating," are a part of the practice of the presence of God. Then into our experience there comes a quieting of the mind and of the thoughts, an opening of the ears as of listening, and occasionally a fleeting breath, or peace, or awareness. Something comes that may last only a second. It may fly by so fast that we wonder if it really happened. It is for this reason that the practice must be continued until eventually we settle down inside into a state of peace. The reason is that by this time we have been able to go within without taking our problems with us, without taking our relatives within, our friends, or our fears of war.

Communion

Eventually we are enabled to go within and leave the world outside. When that happens, we enter a state of communion because the Father knows nothing of these worldly conditions. If He knew about them He would solve them before we ever thought about them, but the kingdom of God is something entirely different from this world: "My kingdom is not of this world." *My* peace is not the peace that the world gives.

After many weeks, we have probably learned this lesson so thoroughly that we can settle into our meditation and immediately leave the world parked outside. Thus we come into communion with the spirit of God that indwells us, that always has been knocking at the door of our consciousness seeking admittance, but now we have admitted It, and now we can commune with It.

What happens in this communion differs so greatly that to each one a different experience comes. There is no use expecting an answer such as your neighbor or fellow student receives. The relationship between you and your Father is such a personal one, such an individual one, that your answer will come in an individual way to fit the needs of your state of consciousness. You may have been ordained to be a healer; you may have been ordained to be an artist, a writer, or an actor.

To each will come an unfoldment in accordance with his individual state of consciousness, because you may be assured that while the human race has no mission, no destiny except to be obliterated, your individual spiritual identity, the Son of God in you which is being raised up in you now, has a specific destiny and purpose that was outlined by God in the beginning when you were created in His image and likeness. While for all these centuries you have been separate and apart from your destiny, in this inner communion you now discover your Self, your true Self, your true Identity, and then your mission is revealed to you, your function on earth, your purpose, and all that is necessary is given to you to fulfill it.

ACROSS THE DESK

Christmas has arbitrarily been set as December 25 and, as with any kind of observance imposed from without, for most persons it has lost its meaning and ceases to play a vital role in the lives of many persons who celebrate that special day. If any of its religious significance is recognized, it is usually in a perfunctory way as a duty.

The real Christmas, which can only be kept in our hearts, is lost sight of, and this is not surprising because to most persons their Christmas Day has not yet come. There has been no inner experience of the Christ in their consciousness. They are asleep to the Light within them which they, in their darkened state of consciousness, do not know or recognize. They do not know that "I am come a light into the world, that whosoever believeth on me should not abide in darkness," and that *I* is within them waiting their recognition. So to the whole world, let us silently and secretly give the Christ-message.

> Awake thou that sleepest, and arise from the dead,
> and Christ shall give thee light.
>
> Ephesians 5:14.

A joyous and blessed Christmas in which the Light within grows ever brighter!

TAPE RECORDED EXCERPTS
Prepared by the Editor

Christmas is a reminder of the universal goal of peace on

earth and good will to men. Can a human being, in and of himself, know the meaning of that good will and Christ-peace? Is not the man of good will the man who has felt the touch of the Christ, by whatever name he calls It, been awakened to Its activity, and consciously has his being in Christ? And does not that man then become an instrument for good will in the world and for the lifting of consciousness universally?

Christmas

"The activity of the Christ in individual consciousness is never for one's own benefit: It is always there as a blessing, as an activity of good for the unenlightened, that is, for those who have not yet had the experience of the conception and birth of the Christ within their own being. . .

"A Christmas message should always be one of peace. Our thoughts turn from the peace that the world is seeking to "My peace," the true peace which, when men are ready to receive it, comes with healing of mind and body. . . Peace is found as we cease warring with the conditions of earth. Peace is realized as we find our union with each other through the experience of God. Peace is achieved as we lay down the armor of flesh, as we put up the sword of defense from the fears and hates of the world. Peace is attained as we behold the Son of God, ruling first our lives, then our relationships with our neighbor. The world is seeking peace out there in the world, but peace is found only in entertaining the Prince of Peace within ourselves. . .

"It is your consciousness and mine that is the true temple of the living God where God, in the form of His Son, the Christ, spiritual identity, abides in Its fullness. . ."

Joel S. Goldsmith, "The Christ on Earth," *The First 1955 Kailua Study Group.*

About the Series

The 1971 through 1981 *Letters* will be published as a series of eleven fine-quality soft cover books. Each book published in the first edition will be offered by Acropolis Books and The Valor Foundation, and can be ordered from either source:

ACROPOLIS BOOKS, INC.
8601 Dunwoody Place
Suite 303
Atlanta, GA 30350-2509
(800) 773-9923
acropolisbooks@mindspring.com

THE VALOR FOUNDATION
1101 Hillcrest Drive
Hollywood, FL 33021
(954) 989-3000
info@valorfoundation.com

Scriptural References and Notes

CHAPTER ONE

[1] I Corinthians 2:14.
[2] Romans 8:17.
[3] Luke 15:31.
[4] Matthew 23:9.
[5] John 10:30.
[6] I John 3:2.
[7] John 8:58.
[8] Psalm 91:1.
[9] Isaiah 2:22.
[10] Matthew 4:4.
[11] Luke 23:34.
[12] John 18:36.
[13] John 14:27.

CHAPTER TWO

[1] Philippians 4:13.
[2] John 18:36.
[3] Luke 12:22.
[4] John 14:27.
[5] I Samuel 3:9.
[6] I Kings 19:12.
[7] Mark 8:18.
[8] Matthew 24:44.
[9] John 10:30.
[10] Psalm 46:10.
[11] John 6:35.
[12] John 10:10.

CHAPTER THREE

[1] John 10:30.
[2] Exodus 3:14.
[3] John 4:32.
[4] John 6:35.
[5] Matthew 4:4.
[6] John 10:10.
[7] John 7:24.
[8] Matthew 10:34.
[9] Matthew 23:9.
[10] 1 Corinthians 3:16.
[11] Luke 22:42.
[12] Psalm 24:1.
[13] Luke 15:31.
[14] Joel 2:25.
[15] John 8:58.
[16] John 18:36.
[17] John 15:6.
[18] I John 4:4.
[19] John 14:10.
[20] John 5:30.

CHAPTER FOUR

[1] Genesis 1:1.
[2] Genesis 1:27.
[3] John 10:10.
[4] John 8:58.
[5] Matthew 28:20.
[6] Romans 8:38, 39.
[7] Matthew 3:17.
[8] John 14:10.
[9] I John 4:4.
[10] John 5:30.
[11] John 18:36.
[12] John 14:27.
[13] Luke 12:31.
[14] John 12:32.
[15] Matthew 26:11.
[16] I Corinthians 2:14.
[17] John 5:30,31.
[18] I Corinthians 15:31

CHAPTER FIVE

[1] Philippians 2:5.
[2] I Corinthians 2:14.
[3] Mark 8:18.
[4] I Kings 19:12.
[5] John 5:30.
[6] Matthew 4:19.
[7] John 1:17.
[8] Galatians 6:7.
[9] Galatians 6:8.
[10] Joel 2:25.
[11] Luke 22:42.
[12] John 5:30,31.
[13] John 14:10.
[14] Job 23:14.
[15] John 10:10.
[16] Genesis 18:32.
[17] Matthew 4:10.
[18] II Corinthians 12:9.
[19] Isaiah 1:18.

CHAPTER SEVEN

[1] Matthew 7:14.
[2] Luke 24:49 (Revised Standard Version).
[3] Galatians 2:20.
[4] Job 23:14.
[5] Philippians 4:13.
[6] Isaiah 45:2.
[7] John 5:30,31.
[8] Matthew 19:17.
[9] Psalm 139:8.
[10] Psalm 23:4.
[11] Luke 23:42.
[12] Romans 8:26.
[13] I Kings 19:18.
[14] Matthew 24:44.
[15] Isaiah 54:17.
[16] Psalm 91:7.
[17] Psalm 91:1.
[18] John 15:5.
[19] John 15:6.
[20] Luke 17:34.
[21] John 10:30.
[22] Luke 15:31.

CHAPTER EIGHT

[1] Luke 12:22.
[2] Luke 12:31.
[3] John 17:20.
[4] John 19:11.
[5] Matthew 5:39.
[6] Isaiah 54:17.
[7] John 8:58.
[8] Matthew 13:24-30.
[9] John 10:30.
[10] II Chronicles 32:8.
[11] Job 23:14.
[12] Matthew 6:10.
[13] Psalm 138:8.
[14] Luke 23:24.
[15] I Thessalonians 5:17.
[16] John 15:4.
[17] John 15:7

CHAPTER NINE

[1] John 5:8.
[2] John 7:24.
[3] John 19:11.
[4] II Chronicles 32:8.
[5] Matthew 16:23.
[6] Isaiah 30:15.
[7] John 14:27.
[8] Philippians 4:7.
[9] John 4:32.
[10] Isaiah 45:2.
[11] John 14:2.
[12] Revelation 21:27.
[13] Hebrews 13:5.
[14] John 6:35.
[15] Luke 17:21.
[16] Matthew 6:10.
[17] Galatians 2:20.
[18] Isaiah 26:3.
[19] Proverbs 3:5,6.

CHAPTER TEN

1 Matthew 28:18.
2 John 10:30.
3 II Chronicles 20:17.
4 Luke 15:31.
5 John 16:33.
6 Matthew 5:39.
7 Isaiah 45:2.
8 Isaiah 2:22.
9 John 14:27.
10 Robert Browning.

CHAPTER ELEVEN

1 Alfred, Lord Tennyson.
2 John 5:8.
3 John 8:58.
4 Matthew 28:20.
5 Hebrews 13:5.
6 Exodus 3:5.
7 John 5:31.
8 Psalm 23:4.
9 Joel 2:25.
10 John 10:30.
11 John 16:7.

CHAPTER TWELVE

1 Philippians 2:5.
2 Matthew 10:34.
3 Matthew 6:27.
4 Matthew 6:33.
5 Luke 12:32.
6 John 18:36.
7 John 14:27.
8 I Kings 19:12.
9 Hebrews 13:5.
10 Matthew 28:20.
11 Luke 15:31.
12 II Corinthians 12:9.
13 Isaiah 45:2.
14 Psalm 23:4.
15 Galatians 2:20.
16 Philippians 4:13.
17 John 8:58.
18 Matthew 26:52.
19 John 19:11.
20 Psalm 37:25
21 Isaiah 54:17.
20 Psalm 37:25.
21 Isaiah 54:17.
22 Isaiah 2:22.
23 I Corinthians 2:14.
24 Luke 23:34.

Joel Goldsmith
Tape Recorded Classes
Corresponding to the
Chapters of this Volume

⌐~

Tape recordings may be ordered from

THE INFINITE WAY
PO Box 2089, Peoria AZ 85380-2089
Telephone 800-922-3195 Fax 623-412-8766

E-mail: infiniteway@earthlink.net
www.joelgoldsmith.com
Free Catalog Upon Request

CHAPTER 12: FULFILLMENT OF SPIRITUAL IDENTITY THROUGH MEDITATION, CONTEMPLATION, AND COMMUNION

#539   1964 Honolulu Infinite Way
         Study Center 3:1